love notes

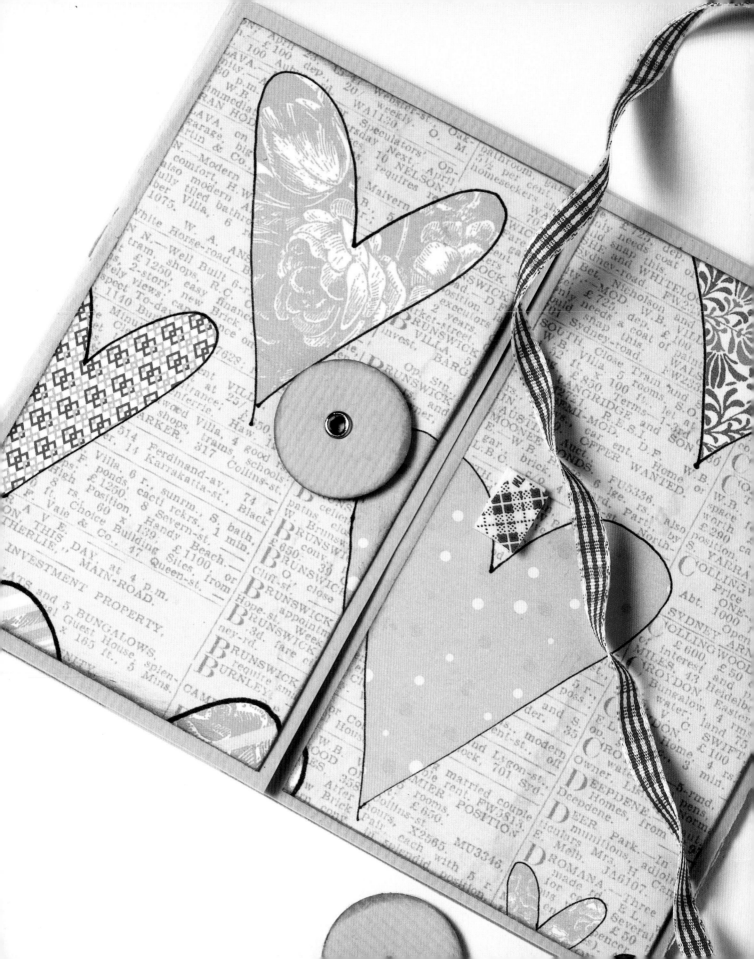

love notes

40 Exquisite Handmade Cards to Express Your Love

edited by

Jan Stephenson & Amy Appleyard

SPARK CRAFT STUDIOS

STERLING/HOLLAN
An imprint of Sterling Publishing Co., Inc.

New York / London
www.sterlingpublishing.com

STERLING and the distinctive Sterling logo are registered trademarks of
Sterling Publishing Co., Inc.

Library of Congress Cataloging-in-Publication Data Available
2 4 6 8 10 9 7 5 3 1

Produced by Hollan Publishing, Inc.
100 Cummings Center, Suite 125G
Beverly, MA 01915

Published by Sterling Publishing Co., Inc.
387 Park Avenue South, New York, NY 10016
© 2007 by Hollan Publishing, Inc.

Distributed in Canada by Sterling Publishing
c/o Canadian Manda Group, 165 Dufferin Street
Toronto, Ontario, Canada M6K 3H6
Distributed in the United Kingdom by GMC Distribution Services
Castle Place, 166 High Street, Lewes, East Sussex, England BN7 1XU
Distributed in Australia by Capricorn Link (Australia) Pty. Ltd.
P.O. Box 704, Windsor, NSW 2756, Australia

Printed in China

Sterling ISBN-13: 978-1-4027-4929-2
ISBN-10: 1-4027-4929-5

For information about custom editions, special sales, premium and
corporate purchases, please contact Sterling Special Sales
Department at 800-805-5489 or specialsales@sterlingpub.com.

HOLLAN
publishing, inc.

Photography by Allan Penn

Cover and interior design by woolypear

To all who create beauty in this world,
be they crafty or not

Introduction 8

CHAPTER 1
Materials and Tools 12

CHAPTER 2
Cards for Lovers 16

You Complete Me	18
Flying High Up on the Wings of Love	20
Love Grows	22
Where I Go	24
Your Love Brings Color to My World	26
Love Potion #9	28
With U I Can Just Be Me	30
Oh Baby!	32
In Love There Is No Measure of Time	34
Be Silly	36
You Have My Heart Tied Up with Love	38
Happy 5th Anniversary	40
Gravitation Is Not Responsible	42
Hot Stuff	44
True Love	46
Love	48
I'm Smitten	50
Woody Allen Quotation	54
XOXO	56
To-Do List	58
The Heart Has Its Reasons	60

CHAPTER 3
Cards for Children 62

Happy Birthday	64
Butterfly Kisses	67
Angel Card	70
You Brighten My Days, Son	72
Li'l Love Bug	74
You Color My World	76

Contents

CHAPTER 4

Cards for Brothers and Sisters 78

Sister Purse Box	80
Top 10 Reasons Why I Love You, Sis	84
Brother	86
Red Sox	88

CHAPTER 5

Cards for Parents and Grandparents 90

Grandma Card	92
To the Best Grandpa	94
Dad, My Hero	96
For You, Mom, with Love	98

CHAPTER 6

Cards for Friends 100

You Bring Out the Best in Me	102
Heartfelt Wishes	104
You Make My World Brighter	106
Love and Chocolate	108
Who I Love	110

CHAPTER 7

Expressions of Love 112

CHAPTER 8

Resources 114

Contributors 122
Acknowledgments 124
Author Biographies 125
Project Gallery 126
Index 128

Introduction

Ah, the love note. Few gifts capture the romantic's imagination so well. Tucked underneath a pillow, nestled inside a favorite book, or slipped under the door, a love note has the ability to quicken our heartbeats and leave us breathless with anticipation.

Generally associated with St. Valentine's Day, love notes first began to appear around the year 1400, becoming popularized in eighteenth-century England, and then spreading to America. Steeped in legend and tradition, love notes remain the quintessential symbol of passion and Cupid's medium of choice. Unlike a lengthy handwritten letter, a love note can be short and sweet, and deliver a powerful punch of adoration. This book will detail all the tools, materials, and techniques you need to create a variety of beautiful handmade cards to express your feelings to the most important people in your life. Love notes are not just for lovers. Handmade cards can also be a gesture of thoughtfulness and close friendship. Thus, many of the love notes you will discover in this book were designed with children, parents, siblings, friends, and other important relations in mind. Imagine how appreciative they will be, knowing that you spent your time and effort thinking of them. That's a rarity in this fast-paced world.

You have my
heart tied up
with love...

Whether you are a new or seasoned papercrafter, feel free to use this book as a source of inspiration as well as a reference guide. You get to choose the style, greeting, and message—be it humorous, heartfelt, or romantic. One of the best things about giving a handmade card is that you can add your own personal touch. You may replicate the cards featured in these pages, or simply use these examples as a jumping-off point for your own creativity. Read the book from start to finish, or refer to the guides and samples from time to time to encourage fresh ideas.

Chapter 1 provides a pictorial overview of the various tools and materials used to complete the cards highlighted in this book. Bring this book with you to your local craft store and use it as a resource to quickly and easily identify the products you will need. Chapter 2 focuses on traditional love notes that are fitting for husbands, wives, boyfriends, and girlfriends. Chapter 3 explores love notes for children, offering ideas for cards that will become cherished keepsakes for daughters, sons, nieces, nephews, and others. Chapters 4, 5, and 6 feature handmade cards appropriate for other loved ones in your life, including siblings, cousins, friends, parents, and grandparents. These cards can also be adapted to include guardians, mentors, aunts, uncles, and other relatives. Of course, any of the designs featured in this book can be adapted to suit the recipient of your card with just a few simple language adjustments.

No matter how intricate the card design, the most important ingredient in a love note is its heartfelt message. Chapter 7 offers thoughts on how to compose your own greetings or find quotations to adorn your handmade cards. It also explores the basic components of writing a thoughtful, personalized message to capture your emotions and shows ways to incorporate handwritten elements, even for those who dislike their own handwriting. Chapter 8 provides a resource guide to help you locate the specific tools and materials cited in this book.

We hope *Love Notes: 40 Exquisite Handmade Cards to Express Your Love* will encourage and guide you through the process of creating handmade cards—a gift with the unique ability to pull at the heartstrings of those you hold dear.

CHAPTER 1

Materials and Tools

The handmade cards featured in *Love Notes* were created using a variety of tools and materials that can be found at your local craft store. Refer to the supply list for each project before shopping for tools and materials to create your cards. Some cards use unique products from a particular manufacturer. Check the Resources section at the end of this book for specific product information. The following section outlines the basic types of tools and materials you will need to create the cards in this book.

MATERIALS

Cardstock and Note Cards

Heavy-weight cardstock or premade blank note cards serve as the base for handmade cards.

Paper and Paper Substitutes

Solid and patterned paper, vellum, metallic paper, clear plastic, fabric, leather, and other paper substitutes add texture and graphic design elements.

Envelopes and Templates

Use white or colored store-bought envelopes in sizes A2, A4, or square, or create your own envelopes using envelope templates.

Adhesives

Liquid glue, glue pens, double-sided tape, tape runners, glue dots, glitter glue, spray adhesive, Fabric-Tac, and foam mounting squares are common adhesives.

Writing and Coloring Instruments

Keep a variety of pencils, journaling pens, colored markers, glitter pens, gel markers, foam markers, and other writing instruments on hand.

Stamps and Ink

Rubber, foam, and acrylic stamps provide images, sentiments, and details you can use on cards again and again. Invest in an array of ink pads, stamping markers, and acrylic paints to color stamped images.

Ribbon and Trimmings

Ribbon, twine, embroidery floss, thread, yarn, and craft wire can add a creative flourish to cards.

Stickers and Rub-ons

Stickers and rub-on transfers come in a variety of colors, sizes, styles, and materials and are perfect for adding words, phrases, or design elements to cards.

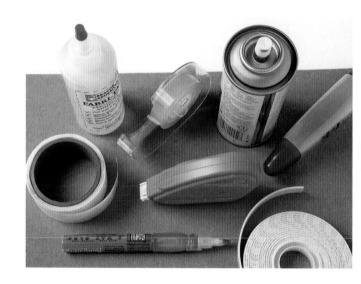

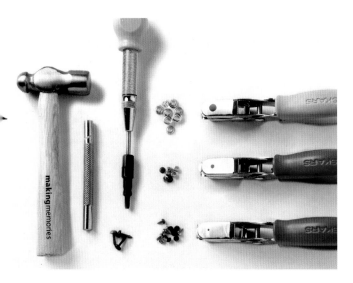

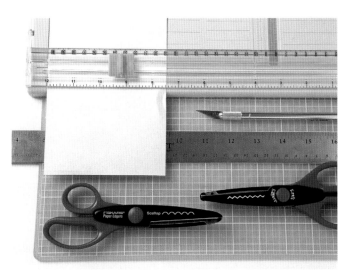

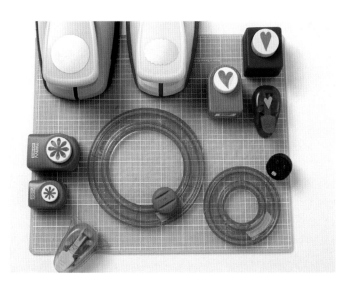

Attachments and Embellishments

Get creative with brads, eyelets, metal-rimmed tags, glitter, staples, safety pins, beads, chipboard (decorated cardboard), and other card accents.

TOOLS

Paper Trimmers

Measure and cut cardstock, paper, and photos with a paper trimmer or use a cutting mat, a ruler, and an X-ACTO knife.

Hole Punchers

Use an awl to make small punctures in cardstock or paper for hand sewing. Hole punches in sizes $\frac{1}{16}$, $\frac{1}{8}$, and $\frac{1}{4}$ inch are commonly used for punching holes for brads and eyelets.

Eyelet-Setting Tools

Invest in an all-in-one universal hole punch/eyelet setter, or use a small hammer, a hole punch, and an eyelet setter.

Scissors

Use regular scissors to cut cardstock and paper and decorative-edged scissors to make scalloped edges and more.

Bone Folder

A bone folder adds a professional-looking crease to score (fold) cardstock into a card base.

Sewing Machine

Quickly and easily add zigzag- or straight-stitch elements to your cards by machine sewing on paper.

Computer and Printer

Create card greetings and messages with word-processing fonts and an inkjet printer.

Cutting Systems and Punches

Cutting systems and handheld punches can be used to cut letters, numbers, and shapes or to round or design card corners.

CHAPTER 2

Cards for Lovers

Love letters—and their offspring, the love note—are as timeless as love itself. Throughout history, they have signaled true passion. And when used sparingly, a well-crafted love note can become your most powerful instrument for saying "I love you" without saying anything at all.

As children, we gave handmade cards and gifts to our favorite people all the time. Even at a young age, we realized that these gifts were something special, reserved for only the most important people in our thoughts. When adults take the time to show their affection in this way, the simple act of making a card takes on a fairy-tale meaning.

Giving your spouse or lover a handmade card is really two gifts in one. There is the tangible gift—the actual card your loved one will hold in his or her hands and treasure for a lifetime. Then there is the intangible gift—an unspoken, inescapable truth—that you love the person so much you were willing to put the inner workings of your mind, heart, and soul on the line.

You might be reading this book to find inspiration for creating a love note worthy of asking someone to marry you. Or you might be looking for a unique way to wish your loved one a happy anniversary or to honor an important birthday. Maybe you need a clever way to say "I'm sorry." Even if it's a "just because" love note you're after, your handcrafted work of art is sure to surprise and delight the recipient.

You Complete Me

by WENDY WHITE

SUPPLIES

Tools

- [ ] paper trimmer
- [ ] cutting mat and knife
- [ ] ruler
- [ ] bone folder
- [ ] 1½-inch circle hole punch
- [ ] ¼-inch hole punch
- [ ] eyelet setter
- [ ] hammer

Materials

- [ ] purple cardstock
- [ ] off-white cardstock
- [ ] light purple alphabet-patterned paper
- [ ] adhesive
- [ ] three ³⁄₁₆-inch silver eyelets
- [ ] hot pink alphabet letter rub-ons or stickers
- [ ] bead chain

Your lover will delight in the ingenuity of the bead chain and the little circle attachment in this adorable hot pink and purple card.

INSTRUCTIONS

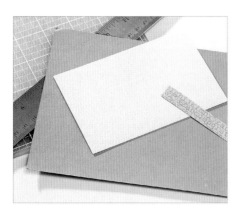

1. With the paper trimmer and a ruler, measure and cut the purple cardstock to 5½ inches tall x 8½ inches wide. Cut the off-white cardstock to 5 inches tall x 3¾ inches wide. Trim the alphabet paper to ½ inch tall x 4¼ inches wide.

2. Fold the purple cardstock in half and score it with a bone folder to create a 5½-inch-tall x 4¼-inch-wide card (it opens from the right).

3. Adhere the alphabet paper strip about one-third of the way down from the top of the front of the card.

4. Use the 1½-inch circle hole punch to punch a circle ½ inch in from the right edge of the card. Save the circle that you punch out.

5. Use the ¼-inch hole punch to make two holes above and below the alphabet paper, to the left of the punched circle. Set eyelets into these holes using the eyelet setter and hammer.

6. Set another eyelet in the top of the punched-out circle.

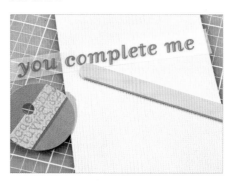

7. Transfer the rub-on word "you" to the alphabet paper on the punched-out circle. Close the card and transfer the rub-on word "me" on the off-white cardstock inside the cutout circle. Open the card and transfer the rub-on word "complete" on the off-white cardstock inside the card. Make sure it lines up with the word "me."

8. Run the bead chain through the eyelets on the card and the eyelet on the circle tag. Snap closed.

Flying High Up on the Wings of Love

by KIMBERLY KESTI

SUPPLIES

Tools

☐ paper trimmer or cutting mat and knife

☐ ruler

☐ bone folder

☐ corner rounder

☐ pencil

☐ scissors

☐ computer with printer and word-processing software

☐ popsicle stick

Materials

☐ light green cardstock

☐ floral-patterned paper

☐ black ink pad

☐ adhesive

☐ black cardstock

☐ white cardstock

☐ wings rub-ons or stickers

☐ foam mounting tape

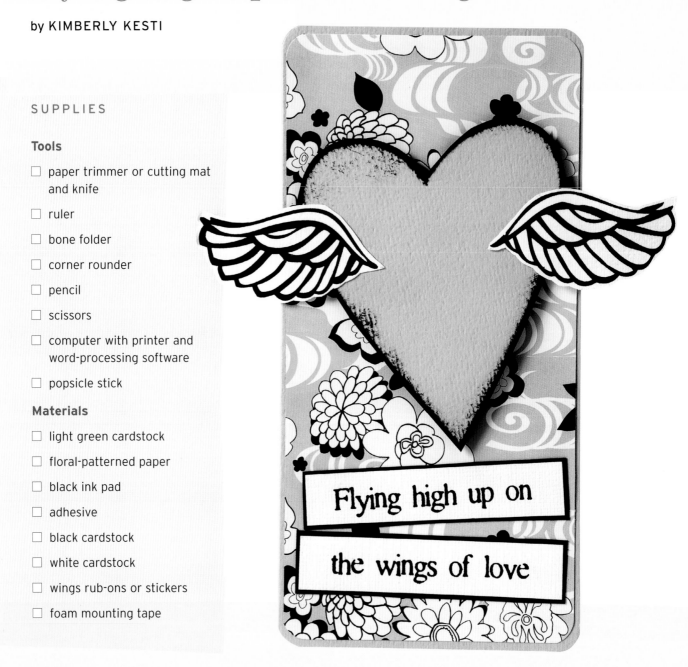

This heart with wings looks as if it's about to fly off the card—creating the perfect metaphor for how your heart soars when you look at your lover.

INSTRUCTIONS

1. With the paper trimmer and ruler, measure and cut the light green cardstock to 7 inches tall x 6 inches wide. Cut the floral paper to 6¾ inches tall x 2¾ inches wide.

2. Fold the light green cardstock in half and score it with a bone folder to create a card 7 inches tall x 3 inches wide (it opens from the right).

3. Round all corners on the cardstock and floral paper with the corner rounder. Adhere floral paper to green card.

4. With pencil, draw a heart on another piece of light green cardstock and cut it out with scissors.

5. Use the black ink pad to ink the edges of the heart.

6. Glue the green heart to the black cardstock. Cut around the edges, leaving a ⅛-inch border to mat the green heart with black cardstock edging.

7. Using a computer and printer, print out your sentiment onto the white cardstock. Cut it into strips, leaving a white border around the text. Mat it onto black cardstock, following the instructions in step 6.

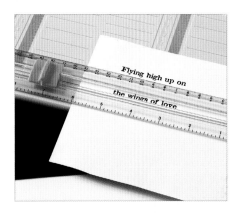

8. Apply the wings rub-ons or stickers to white cardstock, using the popsicle stick to apply pressure. Cut out the wings and adhere them to heart.

9. Adhere the completed heart on the front of the card, using foam mounting tape so the heart "pops" out.

10. Adhere the sentiment strips below the heart.

Love Grows

by WENDY WHITE

Tools

- [ ] paper trimmer or cutting mat and knife
- [ ] ruler
- [ ] bone folder
- [ ] awl and hand-sewing needle
- [ ] sewing machine
- [ ] pencil
- [ ] scissors

Materials

- [ ] white cardstock
- [ ] white paper
- [ ] tree stamp
- [ ] red stamp ink
- [ ] red embroidery floss
- [ ] stickers that spell "LOVE"
- [ ] adhesive
- [ ] handmade red patterned paper for envelope
- [ ] envelope template (5 ¾ inches square)

A bright red tree bursts to life against a snow-white background, symbolizing the growth and burning desires of deep-seated passion.

INSTRUCTIONS

1. With the paper trimmer and ruler, measure and cut the white cardstock to 5 inches tall x 10 inches wide. Fold it and score it with the bone folder to make 5-inch x 5-inch square card (it opens from the right). Cut another piece of white cardstock to 3¼ inches tall x 2¼ inches wide. Cut the white paper to 3 inches tall x 2 inches wide.

2. Stamp a tree image onto the white paper cutout, using red stamp ink. Allow to dry.

3. With the awl, punch holes in the stamped tree where the branches and knots will go. Hand embroider detail onto the tree using red embroidery floss and a hand-sewing needle.

4. Mat the white paper with the tree to the small white cardstock cutout. Machine sew (straight stitch) around the edges of the white paper. Stick "LOVE" stickers to the bottom right corner of the tag. Glue the tag to the front of the card.

5. Turn the handmade paper to the back side and trace the envelope template with a pencil. Cut out the envelope with scissors, fold the edges in, and adhere with glue.

Where I Go

by WENDY WHITE

SUPPLIES

Tools

- [ ] paper trimmer or cutting mat and knife
- [ ] ruler
- [ ] bone folder
- [ ] heart punch
- [ ] computer with printer and word-processing software
- [ ] sewing machine

Materials

- [ ] tan cardstock
- [ ] light green cardstock
- [ ] map-patterned paper
- [ ] red cardstock
- [ ] muted green ink (optional)
- [ ] red heart rub-on, sticker, or die cut (optional)
- [ ] glue

Show your lover how much you'll be missing him or her, whether you're heading out for a day at the office or a trip around the world.

INSTRUCTIONS

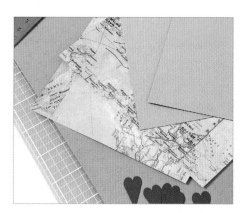

1. With the paper trimmer and ruler, measure and cut the tan cardstock to 7 inches tall x 10 inches wide. Score the tan cardstock with the bone folder to form a card 7 inches tall x 5 inches wide (it opens from the right side). Cut the light green cardstock to 6¾ inches tall x 4¾ inches wide. Cut two pieces of the map-patterned paper, one 6½ inches tall x 4½ inches wide (for the outside) and the other 5½ inches tall x 4½ inches wide (for the inside). Cut a 1¼-inch-tall x 6-inch-wide strip of tan cardstock. Punch nine small hearts from the red cardstock. If you wish, use a muted green ink pad to ink along the edges of the map paper and the green cardstock.

2. Using the word-processing software, type "No matter where I go" in a text box that is 1½ inches tall x 4½ inches wide. Print it onto light green card-stock and trim to 1½ inches tall x 4½ inches wide. Type "my heart stays with you" in a text box that is 5 inches tall x 4½ inches wide. Print it onto light green cardstock and trim to 5 inches tall x 4½ inches wide.

TIP: Leave a space where the word "heart" should be and use a red heart rub-on, sticker, or die cut instead of the typed word.

3. Assemble the card. For the outside, layer the map paper on the light green cardstock and the light green cardstock onto the front of the card. Place the title rectangle on top. Embellish by gluing on a punched heart. For the inside, layer the light green cardstock on the map paper and then adhere to the card.

4. Place eight punched hearts along the ¼-inch strip of tan cardstock. Use a sewing machine (straight stitch) to attach the hearts to the cardstock strip.

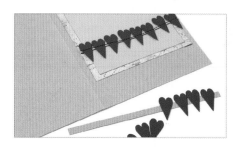

TIP: Add the hearts one at a time and don't worry about lining them up perfectly. Glue the tan strip with hearts to the inside of the card.

Your Love Brings Color to My World

by SUSAN WEINROTH

Festive fabric hearts and playful rhinestones provide a metaphor for the way our hearts burst with color and light when love is in the air.

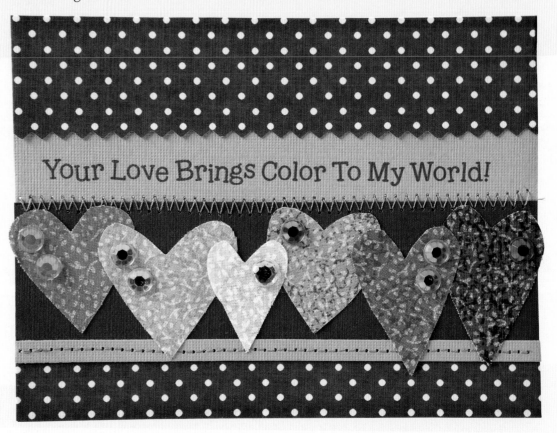

SUPPLIES

Tools

- ☐ paper trimmer or cutting mat and knife
- ☐ ruler
- ☐ bone folder
- ☐ pinking shears
- ☐ computer with printer and word-processing software
- ☐ scissors
- ☐ sewing machine
- ☐ iron

Materials

- ☐ light tan cardstock
- ☐ dark brown polka-dot-patterned paper
- ☐ dark brown cardstock
- ☐ fabric in denim and five other colors
- ☐ fabric glue
- ☐ rhinestones in colors complementary to the fabric
- ☐ tan and brown ribbon (¼ inch wide by 4 inches long)
- ☐ button

INSTRUCTIONS

1. With the paper trimmer and ruler, measure and cut the tan cardstock to 8 inches tall x 5 1/4 inches wide. Score in half with the bone folder for a finished card that is 4 inches tall x 5 1/4 inches wide (the card opens from the bottom). Cut two 1 1/4-inch-tall x 5 1/4-inch-wide strips of patterned paper for the top and bottom of the card. Trim one of the patterned paper strip's edges with pinking shears. Cut a dark brown card-stock strip to 1 1/4 inches tall x 5 1/4 inches wide. Cut an envelope from denim fabric using pinking shears.

2. With the computer and printer, print your sentiment onto tan cardstock. Cut it into a 1 3/4-inch-tall x 5 1/4-inch-wide strip. Adhere the patterned papers to the top and bottom of the card base, with the tan greeting strip and the dark brown strip layered in between.

3. With scissors, cut hearts from fabric in various sizes and shapes. Adhere all but one of the hearts over the dark brown cardstock. Embellish the hearts with colored rhinestones. Use a sewing machine to zigzag stitch underneath the sentiment and straight stitch below the hearts.

4. Fold the denim fabric over where the creases go and press with an iron. Use fabric glue to adhere the sides shut, and then attach four pieces of 1/4-inch-wide x 4-inches-long ribbon so that the brown ribbon overlaps the tan ribbon. Add the button and the last heart accent.

Love Potion #9

by RENÉE DEBLOIS

SUPPLIES

Tools

☐ two sizes of oval scallop punch

☐ scissors

Materials

☐ square pink-dot note card

☐ black ink pad

☐ Love Potion #9 stamp

☐ Boris/Mad Scientist stamp

☐ white cardstock

☐ red cardstock

☐ pink and red markers

☐ liquid glue

☐ two google eyes

☐ mini glue dots

☐ black and white striped ribbon (³⁄₈ inch wide by 9 inches long)

☐ tape

☐ foam mounting tape

☐ Brewing Up Some Fun stamp

Let this mad scientist stir up some good trouble for you when you give this lighthearted card to your lover.

INSTRUCTIONS

1. Situate the square pink-dot note card so that the fold is at the top. Use black ink to stamp a Love Potion #9 image into each of the nine pink circles on the card.

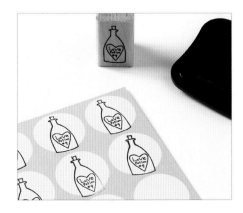

2. Stamp a Mad Scientist image onto white cardstock using black ink. Punch out the image using the smaller of the two oval scallop punches.

TIP: Be sure to center the stamped image by turning the punch upside down to punch. Punch out a larger oval scallop in red cardstock.

3. Color the Mad Scientist with pink and red markers, including drawing hearts coming out of the beakers. Center and glue the smaller white scallop oval to the larger red scallop oval. Attach google eyes with mini glue dots.

4. Wrap the black and white striped ribbon around the card, meeting the ends in the front. Trim the ribbon as needed and tape the ends down. Use foam mounting tape to attach the white/red cardstock ovals to the center of the card. Use black ink to stamp "Brewing Up Some Fun" on the inside bottom right of the card.

With U I Can Just Be Me

by CANDICE CRUZ

SUPPLIES

Tools

- [ ] paper trimmer or cutting mat and knife
- [ ] ruler
- [ ] bone folder
- [ ] heart punch

Materials

- [ ] white cardstock
- [ ] orange cardstock
- [ ] cream cardstock
- [ ] dark green cardstock
- [ ] three shades of blue cardstock
- [ ] adhesive
- [ ] parentheses stamp
- [ ] black ink pad
- [ ] large "U" stamp
- [ ] uppercase alphabet stamps
- [ ] blue watercolor pencil
- [ ] thin paintbrush

Take a cue from the modern style with this hip, informal card that tells it like it is.

INSTRUCTIONS

1. With a paper trimmer and ruler, measure and cut the white cardstock to 7 inches tall x 10 inches wide. Fold and score the white cardstock with a bone folder to create a 7-inch-tall x 5-inch-wide card base (it opens from the right). Cut the other colored card-stocks into ³⁄₄-inch x ³⁄₄-inch squares. You will need a total of 23 squares.

2. Adhere the colored squares to the front of the card in a random color order, starting in the upper left corner. Leave a ¹⁄₈-inch margin between each square.

3. Stamp a large parentheses image in black ink in the bottom right section of the card, making sure you leave room for the rest of the words. Stamp the letter "U" in between the parentheses. Use the alphabet stamps to stamp in the remaining parts of the phrase.

4. Color in the large "U" with a watercolor pencil. Use a thin paintbrush to change the pencil lead into watercolor. Set aside to dry. Punch out a heart shape from a piece of colored cardstock and adhere to the bottom right corner.

Oh Baby!

by CANDICE CRUZ

A picture is worth a thousand words, as this adorable card demonstrates.

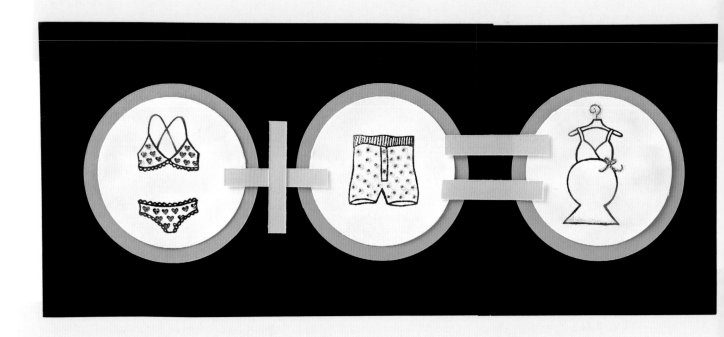

SUPPLIES

Tools

- ☐ 2-inch-diameter circular cutting tool
- ☐ 2 ³/₈-inch-diameter circular cutting tool
- ☐ paper trimmer or cutting mat and knife
- ☐ ruler
- ☐ bone folder
- ☐ scissors

Materials

- ☐ Lingerie stamp
- ☐ Boy Shorts stamp
- ☐ Maternity Dress stamp
- ☐ black ink pad
- ☐ white cardstock
- ☐ black cardstock
- ☐ green cardstock
- ☐ adhesive
- ☐ glue pen
- ☐ glitter
- ☐ yellow cardstock
- ☐ Oh Baby! stamp
- ☐ glassine envelope (4 ¼ inches tall by 9 ½ inches wide)

INSTRUCTIONS

1. Stamp the Lingerie, Boy Shorts, and Maternity Dress rubber stamp images in black ink onto white cardstock. Let the ink dry, and then cut each image into a 2-inch circle with the cutting tool.

2. With the paper trimmer and ruler, measure and cut the black cardstock to 4 inches tall x 18½ inches wide. Fold the cardstock from left to right so the left flap is 6¼ inches. Fold the cardstock from right to left so the right flap is 3¼ inches. Score all folds with the bone folder. Cut three 2⅜-inch-diameter circles out of the green cardstock using cutting tool. Adhere the white circles to the green circles. Apply glue pen to make accents on the stamped images (e.g., hearts on the lingerie, dots on the boy shorts, a bow on the maternity dress). Sprinkle glitter on top of the glue. Shake off the excess glitter. Set aside to dry. When dry, adhere the three green circles onto the front of the card.

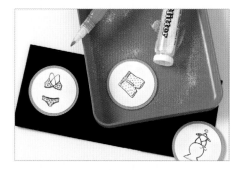

3. Cut the yellow cardstock into four ¼-inch-tall x 1½-inch-wide strips. Adhere two of the yellow strips between the first and second circles to form a plus sign. Adhere two of the yellow strips between the second and third circles to create an equals sign.

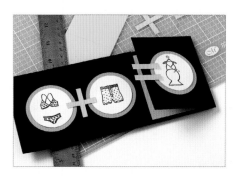

TIP: Only apply adhesive to the right side of each strip of the equals sign so that the flap can still open.

4. Cut the green cardstock to 3½ inches tall x 8½ inches wide and adhere it to the inside center of the card. Cut green cardstock to 3½ inches tall x 3 inches wide and stamp "Oh Baby!" in the center. Adhere it to the inside right flap. Let dry, then place in the glassine envelope.

In Love There Is No Measure of Time

by KIMBERLY KESTI

SUPPLIES

Tools

☐ paper trimmer or cutting mat and knife

☐ ruler

☐ ¼-inch hole punch

☐ bone folder

☐ sewing machine

☐ computer with printer and word-processing software

Materials

☐ pink cardstock

☐ white lined, scallop-edged paper

☐ pink and white striped paper

☐ adhesive

☐ white cardstock

☐ clock embellishment

☐ flat-backed rhinestones

☐ pink ribbon with white dashed lines (⅛ inch wide by 4 inches long)

☐ red heart-in-a-circle embellishment

☐ glue dots

Sow the seeds of love and capture the timelessness of passion with this fabulous gem of a card.

INSTRUCTIONS

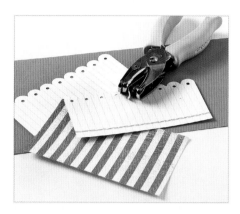

1. With the paper trimmer and ruler, measure and cut pink cardstock to 11 inches tall x 5 inches wide. Cut two 2½-inch-tall x 5-inch-wide pieces of scallop-edged paper. Cut a 3½-inch-tall x 5-inch-wide piece of pink and white striped paper.

2. Use the ¼-inch hole punch to punch holes in each of the scalloped edges on the paper.

3. Fold the pink cardstock in half (from the top down) and score with the bone folder to create a card 5½ inches tall x 5 inches wide (it opens from the bottom).

4. Adhere the scallop-edged paper to the front of the card. Leave ¾ inch of pink cardstock showing at the top and bottom. The scalloped edges should face out. The two pieces of paper will overlap.

5. Adhere the pink and white striped paper in the center on top of the scallop-edged paper.

6. Machine stitch (zigzag stitch) where the pink and white striped paper and the scallop-edged paper meet.

7. Using the computer and printer, print your sentiment onto plain white cardstock. Trim to 1¾ inches tall x 3½ inches wide. Adhere the sentiment to the card on the right side. Machine stitch (zigzag stitch) where the sentiment and pink and white striped paper meet (top and bottom).

8. Assemble the clock: Adhere rhinestones to the clock face, tie the ribbon to the heart embellishment, and use glue dots to adhere the heart to the clock face.

9. Adhere the clock to the front of the card, covering the left edge of the printed sentiment.

Be Silly

by CANDICE CRUZ

SUPPLIES

Tools

☐ paper trimmer or cutting mat and knife

☐ ruler

☐ bone folder

☐ corner rounder

☐ pencil

☐ X-ACTO knife

☐ old mouse pad

☐ awl and hand-sewing needle

☐ computer with printer and word-processing software or writing implement

☐ scissors

Materials

☐ white cardstock

☐ black cardstock

☐ blue cardstock

☐ green cardstock

☐ yellow cardstock

☐ tape

☐ white embroidery floss

☐ chipboard alphabets

Anyone can be passionate, but it takes real lovers to

Be Silly

- Rose Franken

The winding nonsensical patterns on this card represent perfectly the wish to be silly with your lover.

INSTRUCTIONS

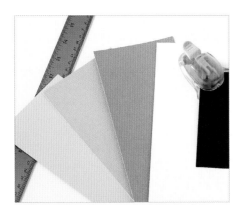

1. With the paper trimmer and ruler, measure and cut a piece of white cardstock to 7 inches tall x 10 inches wide. Fold and score with the bone folder to form a 7-inch-tall x 5-inch-wide card (it opens from the right). Cut a piece of black cardstock to 7 inches tall x 5 inches wide. Round the corners of the white and black cardstocks using a corner rounder tool.

2. Turn the black cardstock over. With a pencil, draw three curvy shapes. Cut each shape out using an X-ACTO knife and cutting mat. Cut pieces of the blue, green, and yellow cardstocks just large enough to cover the curvy shapes. Tape the three pieces to the back of the black cardstock.

3. Turn the black cardstock over so that the good side is facing up. Place it on a cushy surface such as an old mouse pad. Using an awl, poke holes along the edges of the three curvy shapes, leaving about ½ inch between each shape. Create the holes for a leafy stem accent, if desired.

4. Separate two strands of embroidery floss from the skein and thread the needle. Starting on the back side of the cardstock, create the outer stitches of each curvy shape. Go back and connect the holes across each shape. Secure the ends of the embroidery floss on the back of the card with a piece of tape.

5. Using a computer and printer, print the quotation onto a piece of white cardstock (or handwrite it). Cut out each word with scissors and adhere them to the right side of the card in a random pattern.

6. Adhere the "Be Silly" chipboard letters at the bottom of the card.

7. Adhere the black cardstock to the front of the white card base.

You Have My Heart Tied Up with Love

by KIMBERLY KESTI

This whimsical card cheerfully illustrates how love can take hold of your heart.

SUPPLIES

Tools

- [ ] paper trimmer or cutting mat and knife
- [ ] ruler
- [ ] bone folder
- [ ] 1-inch-diameter circle punch
- [ ] ⅛-inch hole punch
- [ ] eyelet setter and hammer

Materials

- [ ] light blue cardstock
- [ ] heart on newsprint-patterned paper
- [ ] adhesive
- [ ] purple ink pad (optional)
- [ ] two ⅛-inch silver eyelets

- [ ] journaling pen
- [ ] foam mounting tape
- [ ] red gingham ribbon (¼ inch wide by 15 inches long)

INSTRUCTIONS

1. With the paper trimmer and ruler, measure and cut the light blue cardstock to 5 inches tall x 12 inches wide. Gatefold and score with the bone folder so the left and right flaps are 3 inches wide and the card opens in the middle. Cut two pieces of the newsprint-patterned paper to 4 3/4 inches tall x 2 3/4 inches wide. Glue the patterned paper to the left and right flaps. Punch two 1-inch circles from light blue cardstock using the circle punch. If you wish, ink the circle edges with purple stamp ink.

2. In each circle, punch 1/8-inch holes for eyelets. Set a silver eyelet into the center of each circle using the eyelet setter and hammer.

3. Write your sentiment on the inside of the card with a journaling pen.

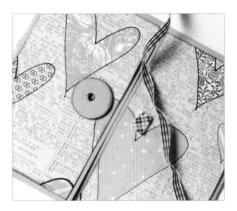

4. Use the foam mounting tape to adhere the circles to the center of the card front on either side of the gatefold. Tie the card closed with the red gingham ribbon.

Happy 5th Anniversary

by RENÉE DEBLOIS

SUPPLIES

Tools

- [ ] paper trimmer or cutting mat and knife
- [ ] ruler
- [ ] scissors
- [ ] computer with printer and word-processing software
- [ ] sewing machine
- [ ] ⅛-inch hole punch

Materials

- [ ] neutral cardstock
- [ ] fabric that has man and woman and bird images
- [ ] ink-jet transparency sheet
- [ ] spray adhesive
- [ ] mini dot adhesive
- [ ] ivory thread
- [ ] pop dot adhesive
- [ ] two black brads

A toile fabric swatch makes a beautiful card to wish your lover a happy anniversary.

INSTRUCTIONS

1. With the paper trimmer and ruler, measure and cut two pieces of neutral cardstock to 7 inches tall x 5 inches wide. With scissors, cut the top corners at an angle to create a tag shape. Situate the fabric on the tag so the image of the man and woman sits in the lower left. Cut to size. Cut out two birds from the fabric.

2. Using the computer and word-processing software, create a 7-inch-tall x 5-inch-wide text box. Write your sentiment and move words into position. Print the words onto an ink-jet transparency sheet, let dry, and cut to 7 inches tall x 5 inches wide.

3. Use spray adhesive to adhere the fabric to the tag. When dry, cut off excess fabric around the tag. Position the transparency over the fabric-covered tag. Use mini glue dots at the four corners to temporarily hold the transparency in place.

HINT: First roll the glue dots between two fingers to make them less sticky.

4. Use a sewing machine with ivory thread (zigzag stitch) to attach the transparency to the front of the card.

TIP: Remove the glue dots before the needle strikes. Cut off any excess pieces of transparency.

5. Use spray adhesive to adhere the fabric bird images to a piece of cardstock. When dry, cut around the edges of the birds so you have two birds backed with cardstock. Adhere the bird cutouts to the front of the card with pop dots so they stand out.

6. Use the $1/8$-inch hole punch to make two holes at the top of the tag. Attach the black brads.

Gravitation Is Not Responsible

by CANDICE CRUZ

Hearts fall from the sky in this cheerful mosaic love note.

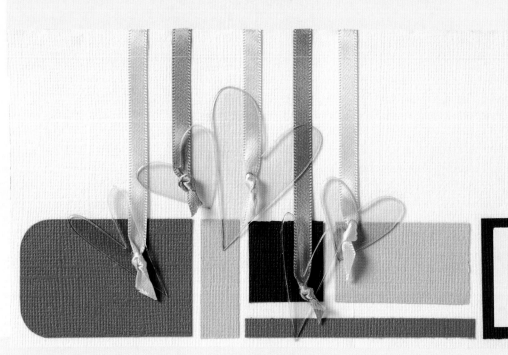

gravitation is not
responsible for people
falling in love.
- albert einstein

SUPPLIES

Tools

- [ ] paper trimmer or
  cutting mat and knife
- [ ] ruler
- [ ] bone folder
- [ ] corner rounder
- [ ] computer with printer and word-
  processing software
- [ ] ⅛-inch hole punch

Materials

- [ ] white cardstock
- [ ] three different shades of
  blue cardstock
- [ ] white paper
- [ ] adhesive

- [ ] plastic hearts
- [ ] yellow and orange ribbon
  (¼ inch wide by 5 inches long)
- [ ] mini glue dots

INSTRUCTIONS

1. With the paper trimmer and ruler, measure and cut the white cardstock to 8 inches tall x 9 inches wide. Fold it in half and score with the bone folder to form a 4-inch-tall x 9-inch-wide card (it opens from the bottom). Cut the light blue cardstock into two pieces, one 1½ inches tall x ½ inch wide and the other 1 inch tall x 1¾ inches wide. Cut the medium-blue cardstock into two pieces, one 1½ inches tall x 2¼ inches wide and the other ¼ inch tall x 3 inches wide. Cut the dark blue cardstock into two pieces, one 1 inch x 1 inch square and the other 1½ inches tall x 2¼ inches wide.

2. Round the top and bottom left corners of the larger medium-blue cardstock. Round the top and bottom right corners of the larger dark blue cardstock. Using the computer and printer, print the quotation onto a piece of white paper. Cut it to 1¼ inches tall x 2½ inches wide. Round the upper and lower right corners, then adhere it to the larger dark blue cardstock. Adhere the pieces of blue cardstock along the bottom of the card in a mosaic fashion, leaving ¼ inch between each piece.

3. Punch a hole in the center of each plastic heart. With scissors, cut three pieces of ¼-inch-wide x 5-inches-long yellow ribbon and two pieces of ¼-inch-wide x 5-inches-long orange ribbon.

4. Tie a knot at the end of the ribbon pieces. Thread the non-knotted ends through the holes in the tops of the plastic hearts. Use a mini glue dot to adhere the ribbon at the top of the card and behind the knots to secure the hearts to the front of the card. Vary placement of the hearts so that they hang at different heights. Trim any excess ribbon from the top of the card.

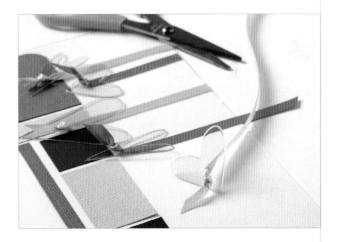

Hot Stuff

by SUSAN WEINROTH

Your lover is sizzling hot, so why not say so with this flirty, animal-print card?

SUPPLIES

Tools

☐ paper trimmer or cutting mat and knife

☐ ruler

☐ computer with printer and word-processing software

☐ scissors

Materials

☐ white cardstock

☐ zebra-patterned paper

☐ black and white striped paper

☐ pink print paper

☐ adhesive

☐ black ribbon
(³⁄₈ inch wide by 6 inches long)

☐ pink cardstock

☐ square metal-rimmed tag

☐ pop dots or foam mounting tape

INSTRUCTIONS

1. With the paper trimmer and ruler, measure and cut the white cardstock to 8 inches tall x 5½ inches wide. Fold and score cardstock to create card base 4 inches tall x 5½ inches wide (opens from the bottom). Cut the zebra paper to 2¾ inches tall x 5½ inches wide. Cut the black and white striped paper to ½ inch tall x 5½ inches wide. Cut the pink print paper to 1 inch tall x 5½ inches wide.

2. Adhere the zebra print paper to the upper two-thirds of the front of the card. Adhere the pink print paper to the bottom, and adhere the thin strip of black and white striped paper above the pink print paper. Adhere the ribbon strip to the top of the black and white striped paper.

3. Create the "Hot Stuff" tag on the computer by reverse printing the text on a black background with white lettering. Print it onto the pink cardstock so the text comes out pink, not white, with a black background. Trim the cardstock to size and insert it into the metal-rimmed tag.

4. Use pop dots or foam mounting tape to adhere the tag to the card.

True Love

by KIMBERLY KESTI

SUPPLIES

Tools

☐ paper trimmer or cutting mat and knife

☐ ruler

☐ pencil

☐ heat embossing tool

☐ pushpin

Materials

☐ black cardstock

☐ striped paper

☐ glue stick

☐ "LOVE" stamp

☐ lavender ink pad

☐ white cardstock

☐ clear embossing powder

☐ jeweled brad

☐ "true" tag

This bejeweled heart reminds your lover that there's nothing as precious as your love for each other.

INSTRUCTIONS

1. With the paper trimmer and ruler, measure and cut a piece of black cardstock to 5 inches tall x 10 inches wide. Fold the cardstock in half from left to right and cut a heart shape, leaving about 2 3/4 inches from the bottom left edge as your hinge.

2. Place the heart-shaped card on top of the patterned paper and trace a heart of equal size. Cut the patterned paper along your trace lines and use a glue stick to adhere the patterned heart to the card front.

3. Stamp "LOVE" in lilac ink on plain white paper. Sprinkle clear embossing powder onto the wet ink. Shake the excess powder from the stamped image. Use the heat embossing tool to heat set the powder.

4. When the powder is dry, cut around the stamped image to make a rectangle that's 2 inches tall x 3 inches wide. Using a pushpin, make a hole near the center of the stamped image and attach the "true" tag with the jeweled brad. Use the glue stick to position the tag horizontally above the word "LOVE." Cut out a piece of black cardstock that's 2 1/8 inches tall x 3 1/8 inches wide. Use the glue stick to mount the white rectangle on the black rectangle. Use the glue stick to adhere the black rectangle to the front of the card.

Love

by KIMBERLY KESTI

Your best friend and lover holds the key to your heart, so give a tangible representation of your devotion.

SUPPLIES

Tools

- [ ] paper trimmer or cutting mat and knife
- [ ] ruler
- [ ] bone folder
- [ ] heat embossing tool
- [ ] scissors
- [ ] corner rounder

Materials

- [ ] red cardstock
- [ ] striped and floral-patterned papers in coordinating colors
- [ ] black patterned paper
- [ ] adhesive
- [ ] alphabet stamps to spell "love"
- [ ] black ink pad
- [ ] tan cardstock
- [ ] clear embossing powder
- [ ] black cardstock
- [ ] foam mounting tape
- [ ] Friend ribbon (⅜ inch wide by 15 inches long)
- [ ] small key embellishment
- [ ] small safety pin

INSTRUCTIONS

1. With the paper trimmer and ruler, measure and cut the red cardstock to 5 inches tall x 10 inches wide. Fold it and score with a bone folder to create a 5-inch-tall x 5-inch-wide square note card (it opens from the right). Cut four 1-inch-tall x 5-inch-wide strips from the striped and floral-patterned papers. Adhere them to the front of the card, leaving a little space between each one so the red cardstock shows through.

2. Stamp the word "love" with black ink onto the tan cardstock. Sprinkle on clear embossing powder and tap off the excess. Use the heat embossing tool to heat set the powder. When dry, trim around the letters with scissors.

3. Cut a 3½-inch square from the black patterned paper. Mat it on a 3½-inch square of black cardstock and round the corners. Adhere it to the front center of the card. Adhere the word "love" to the front of the card with foam mounting tape.

4. Tie the ribbon around the folded edge of the card. Attach the key to the ribbon with a safety pin.

I'm Smitten

by RENÉE DEBLOIS

Your lover will find this unusual card a treat to discover as it unravels its charms bit by bit.

Tools

☐ scissors

☐ ruler

☐ 2½-inch circle punch

☐ sandpaper

☐ sponge brush

☐ paper trimmer or cutting mat and knife

☐ pencil

☐ universal hole punch, and ⅛-inch hole punch, mitten punch tool

Materials

☐ coordinating patterned paper

☐ adhesive

☐ ribbon spool cardboard core (approximately 1 inch tall by 2¾ inches wide)

☐ acrylic paint

☐ two 4-inch-diameter round coasters

☐ large letter stickers

☐ ribbon (⅜ inch wide by 2 feet long)

☐ tape

☐ brown brads

☐ button

1. With scissors and a ruler, measure and cut four
    4-inch-diameter circles from the patterned paper
    and adhere them to cover the coasters front and
    back. Cut six 2 ½-inch circles out of patterned
    paper with the circle punch.

2. Sand the ribbon spool rims to smooth the edges.
    Paint the rims and interiors with acrylic paint and a
    sponge brush. Set aside to dry. With the paper
    trimmer, cut a strip of patterned paper to cover the
    outside of the ribbon spool and adhere the paper
    after the spool has dried. Center and glue the rib-
    bon spool to one of the coasters.

3. Affix the alphabet letters. Place the word "I'M" on the top side of one coaster. Place the letters to form "SMITTE" on each of the six 2½-inch circles. Place the letter "N" inside the second coaster.

4. Mark the center of each coaster with a pencil and ruler. Punch a ¼-inch hole in the center of each coaster using a universal hole punch. Feed one end of ribbon through the bottom hole and tape it underneath.

5. Lay the ribbon outside the bottom coaster and space the six circles along the ribbon. Use the ⅛-inch hole punch to punch a hole into the top of each circle and the ribbon together.

Affix the circles to the ribbon using brown brads.

6. Pull the remaining ribbon end through the top coaster, leaving enough ribbon so that the lid with "I'M" can sit flat next to the "S" without overlapping. Tie a looped knot of the ribbon on the top of the lid to create a handle. Trim off the excess ribbon. Cut out two mittens from the patterned paper with the mitten punch tool. Adhere the mitten cutouts below "I'M" and the button to the left of "I'M."

Woody Allen Quotation

by CANDICE CRUZ

Take a humorous approach to showing your love with this witty card.

"I was nauseous and tingly all over. I was either in love or I had smallpox." - Woody Allen

SUPPLIES

Tools

- [ ] paper trimmer or cutting mat and knife
- [ ] ruler
- [ ] bone folder
- [ ] sandpaper
- [ ] computer with printer and word-processing program
- [ ] heart punch
- [ ] $\frac{1}{16}$-inch hole punch

Materials

- [ ] green cardstock
- [ ] floral-patterned paper
- [ ] cream cardstock
- [ ] adhesive
- [ ] 19 mini brads

INSTRUCTIONS

1. With the paper trimmer and ruler, measure and cut the green cardstock to 8 inches tall x 9 inches wide. Fold it in half and score with the bone folder to form a 4-inch-tall x 9-inch-wide card (it opens from the bottom). Cut the floral paper to 2½ inches tall x 9 inches wide.

2. Crumple up the floral paper and flatten it out again. Use a piece of sandpaper to rub the surface and reveal a bit of the paper's white core.

3. With a computer and printer, print the quotation onto a piece of cream cardstock and trim it to ½ inch tall x 9 inches wide. Adhere it to the card so that there is about 1 inch of green cardstock above.

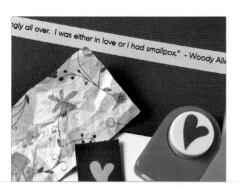

4. Cut a piece of green cardstock to 2½ inches tall x 1½ inches wide. Punch a heart out of the center. Tear a little bit off the bottom edge. Mat it on 1¾-inch-tall x 1¼-inch-wide cream cardstock.

5. Adhere the heart piece to the floral paper about ½ inch in from the right edge and along the top edge.

6. Use the ¹⁄₁₆-inch hole punch to make 19 holes along the top of the floral paper. Insert the mini brads into the holes.

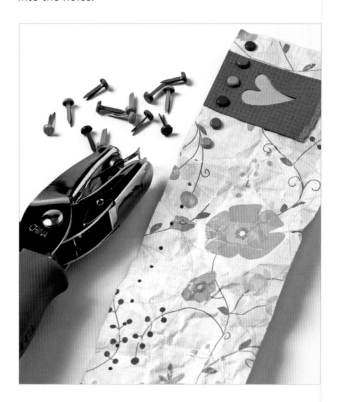

7. Adhere the completed floral paper piece to the bottom of the card.

XOXO

by CANDICE CRUZ

SUPPLIES

Tools

- [ ] cutting mat and knife
- [ ] ruler
- [ ] bone folder
- [ ] small heart punch
- [ ] ¼-inch hole punch
- [ ] eyelet-setting tool and hammer

Materials

- [ ] pink cardstock
- [ ] cream cardstock
- [ ] adhesive
- [ ] silver eyelet
- [ ] red ribbon (¼ inch wide by 6 inches long)
- [ ] XOXO stamp
- [ ] black ink pad
- [ ] three pieces of coordinating ribbon (¼ inch wide by 10 inches long)

Simple and sweet, this card gives kisses and hugs while coyly asking for the favor to be returned.

INSTRUCTIONS

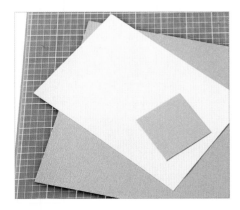

1. With the cutting mat, knife, and ruler, measure and cut the pink cardstock to 7 inches tall x 10 inches wide. Fold it in half and score with the bone folder to form a 7-inch-tall x 5-inch-wide card (it opens on the right).

2. Cut the cream cardstock to 6½ inches tall x 4½ inches wide.

3. Unfold the pink card base and lay it flat on a cutting mat. With a knife, cut a diagonal line from the middle (fold) of the card to the right edge of the card, 3 inches down from the top right corner.

4. Turn the card over so that the inside of the card is facing up. Apply adhesive to the left edge and bottom left edge of the card. Close the card and press firmly over the sides that the adhesive was applied to. This will create a pocket for the cream cardstock to sit inside.

5. Cut the top two corners of the cream cardstock at a diagonal about 1 inch in to create a tag.

6. Punch out a heart from the small piece of pink cardstock. Adhere it to the top of the cream cardstock.

7. Use the ¼-inch hole punch tool to make a hole through the center of the heart and through the cardstock. Set an eyelet into the hole with the eyelet-setting tool and hammer.

8. Tie a piece of ribbon to the cardstock, then insert the cardstock tag into the card pocket.

9. Stamp the "XOXO" message in black ink on the bottom right corner of the front of the card.

10. Starting at the back, wrap three pieces of coordinating ribbon around the card along the bottom. Tie off in front of card so the knots sit in different spots along the card. Cut the ribbon ends on a diagonal.

To-Do List

by WENDY WHITE

SUPPLIES

Tools

- ☐ paper trimmer or cutting mat and knife
- ☐ ruler
- ☐ bone folder
- ☐ ⅛-inch hole punch
- ☐ computer with printer and word-processing software

Materials

- ☐ orange cardstock
- ☐ striped paper
- ☐ green cardstock
- ☐ white cardstock
- ☐ lightly lined notebook paper
- ☐ kraft cardstock
- ☐ adhesive
- ☐ orange grosgrain ribbon (³⁄₈ inch wide x 4 inches long)
- ☐ craft wire

The matter-of-fact nature of the outside text disguises the sexy message within.

INSTRUCTIONS

1. With the paper trimmer and ruler, measure and cut the orange cardstock to 5¼ inches tall x 11½ inches wide. Fold it 6 inches from the left and 1 inch from the right and score it with the bone folder. Cut a 5¼-inch-tall x 2½-inch-wide strip of striped paper. Cut a 5¼-inch-tall x 1-inch-wide strip of green cardstock. Cut a 5¼-inch-tall x ½-inch-wide strip of white cardstock. Cut three pieces of lined notebook paper and one piece of kraft cardstock to 4 inches tall x 3 inches wide.

2. Fold the striped paper strip to cover the right flap and adhere it to the card. Adhere the green cardstock strip on top of the striped paper, flush with the right edge of the right flap. Fold the white cardstock into a "ribbon" strip and then tie orange ribbon around it

3. Use a computer and printer to print "To-Do List" information onto the notebook paper. Paper tear the bottom edge of that piece of lined notebook paper. Hold all three pieces of notebook paper and kraft cardstock together and punch ⅛-inch holes along the top edge.

4. Loop the craft wire around the holes at the top to create a notebook spiral.

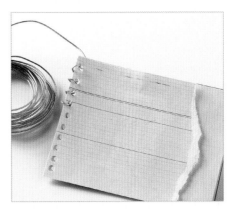

5. Adhere the completed "To-Do List" embellishment to the front of the card, and then slip the white "ribbon" accent over the right-hand side of the card.

TIP: The right flap with the striped paper should be showing on the front of the card.

6. Print the inside message with a black border onto orange cardstock. Cut the cardstock 5 inches x 5 inches and adhere it to the inside of the card.

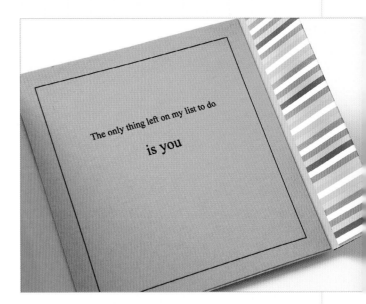

The Heart Has Its Reasons

by RENÉE DEBLOIS

SUPPLIES

Tools

- [ ] paper trimmer or cutting mat and knife
- [ ] ruler
- [ ] bone folder
- [ ] computer with printer and word-processing software

Materials

- [ ] white cardstock
- [ ] red cardstock
- [ ] photo paper
- [ ] spray adhesive
- [ ] red and silver seed beads
- [ ] mini glue dots

Spelled out in black and white with red all over, this big heart spells big love.

INSTRUCTIONS

3. Spray the back of the photo paper with a heavy coat of adhesive and adhere it to the white card-stock card.

4. Spray adhesive onto the red heart. Pour red and silver seed beads onto the heart. Fill in areas as necessary. Let dry overnight. Affix the heart to the card using glue dots.

1. With the paper trimmer and ruler, cut the white cardstock to 11 inches tall x 5½ inches wide. Fold it in half and score with the bone folder to make a 5½-inch square card (it opens from the bottom). Cut a 3-inch-tall x 4-inch-wide heart from red cardstock.

2. Create a 5-inch x 5-inch square text box with the computer and word-processing software. Format the box with a black background (fill color) and white text. Type in the quotation and move the text to the bottom of the box. Print the box onto photo paper and let dry. Cut the box into a 5¼-inch square.

CHAPTER 3

Cards for Children

Remember the magic of finding Mom's handwritten note on the napkin tucked inside your lunchbox? Now you realize the significance of that simple gesture. In the midst of a crazy morning routine, somehow Mom took the time to show you that she loved you. That subtle reminder—that you were not alone—stayed with you the rest of the day.

Sure, there is a good possibility that any child to whom you give a love note will toss the card aside to rip into your gift, or shrug it off and run to play with friends. However, do not underestimate the power of a handmade card given to a child.

Your love note will find its way into that shoebox that sits on the top shelf of the closet or under the bed. Years later, when the child is much older, mementos such as your handmade card will trigger childhood memories and offer tangible proof of your love and affection.

You can create handmade cards for any child who is important in your life—your own children, nieces and nephews, grandchildren, a close friend's child, even students, if you are a teacher or Scout leader. You will find there are many occasions suitable for a love note, but everyday notes can be incredibly meaningful, too. A love note given at an unexpected moment can provide more happiness and encouragement than you could ever imagine.

Happy Birthday

by RENÉE DEBLOIS

Any young girl will adore this butterfly bracelet and fanciful card—a gift and a card rolled into one.

SUPPLIES

Tools

- ☐ paper trimmer or cutting mat and knife
- ☐ ruler
- ☐ bone folder
- ☐ sewing machine
- ☐ flower punch
- ☐ sandpaper
- ☐ universal hole punch with buttonhole and ⅛-inch attachments
- ☐ tapestry needle
- ☐ two sizes of circle punches
- ☐ crimping pliers
- ☐ pencil
- ☐ scissors

Materials

- ☐ white cardstock
- ☐ floral paper
- ☐ adhesive
- ☐ hot pink paper
- ☐ cream-colored thread
- ☐ light pink fabric flower embellishment

- ☐ hot pink embroidery floss
- ☐ white button
- ☐ mini glue dots
- ☐ pink mailbox tile "O"
- ☐ green chipboard "X"
- ☐ green yarn
- ☐ pink cardstock
- ☐ outline of a flower stamp
- ☐ hot pink stamp pad

- ☐ green cardstock
- ☐ Happy Birthday stamp
- ☐ black stamp pad
- ☐ green, silver, pink, and pearl seed beads
- ☐ bead stringing material
- ☐ silver butterfly charm
- ☐ small silver toggle clasp
- ☐ two crimp beads, craft wire, and tape

INSTRUCTIONS

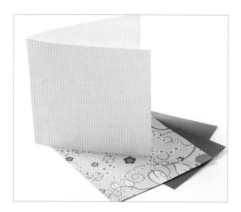

1. With the paper trimmer and ruler, measure and cut the white cardstock to 5 1/4 inches tall x 11 inches wide. Fold it in half and score it with the bone folder to make a 5 1/4-inch-tall x 5 1/2-inch-wide card (it opens to the right). Cut the floral paper to 5 1/4 inches tall x 5 1/2 inches wide. Adhere it to the front of the cardstock.

2. Cut a piece of hot pink paper to 5 1/4 inches tall x 3 inches wide. Tear the edge so that you have a piece measuring 5 1/4 inches tall x 3/4 inch wide. Adhere it to the left front of the card alongside the fold.

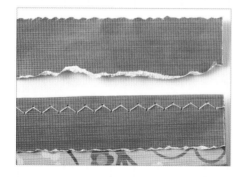

3. Zigzag stitch over the hot pink paper using cream-colored thread and a sewing machine.

4. Assemble the flower accent: Punch out a hot pink flower and layer it on top of the light pink fabric flower embellishment. Tie hot pink embroidery floss through the buttonholes of the white button. Use mini glue dots to layer the flower parts and adhere it to the bottom right of the card.

5. Distress the pink mailbox tile "O" by sanding the top and edges. Adhere the chipboard "X" to the bottom left of the card. Adhere the "O" to the right of this "X."

6. Punch four 1/8-inch holes between the "O" and the pink flower to form an X. Using a tapestry needle and green yarn, create an X by pulling yarn through the holes. Tie off inside the card.

7. Punch buttonholes along the folded side of the card. Sew a line of yarn using these holes and the backstitch.

8. Punch a circle out of pink cardstock. Stamp flowers in hot pink ink. Ink along the edge of the circle with hot pink ink, if desired. Punch a larger circle out of green cardstock and mount the pink circle to it. Stamp "happy" and "birthday" in the center of the pink circle with black ink.

9. String pink, green, silver, and pearl seed beads onto the stringing material. Place the butterfly charm in the center. Crimp the toggle clasp to the ends of the bracelet using the crimp beads and the crimping pliers.

10. Lay the bracelet onto the green and pink "happy birthday" circle. Mark with pencil dots every 90 degrees to punch buttonholes for fastening the bracelet to the card.

11. Punch four sets of buttonholes. Attach the bracelet to the card using craft wire. Twist the wire inside the card. Trim the ends with scissors and tape down.

12. Cut a 5-inch x 5-inch square from pink cardstock. Adhere it to the inside of the card to hide the yarn and craft wire.

Butterfly Kisses

by WENDY WHITE

SUPPLIES

Tools

- [ ] paper trimmer or cutting mat and knife
- [ ] ruler
- [ ] bone folder
- [ ] scissors
- [ ] popsicle stick
- [ ] butterfly lift paper punch

Materials

- [ ] natural cardstock
- [ ] tan cardstock
- [ ] ivory cardstock
- [ ] floral-patterned paper
- [ ] pink dotted ribbon (⅛ inches wide by 8 inches long)
- [ ] alphabet rub-ons
- [ ] clear glitter glue
- [ ] butterfly kisses chipboard sentiment
- [ ] adhesive

Your love for your daughter—delicate and sweet—will shine through with this ethereal, intricately designed card.

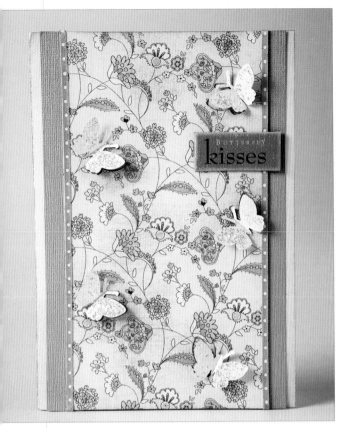

DADDY'S GIRL

1. With the paper trimmer and ruler, measure and cut the natural cardstock to 7 inches tall x 10 inches wide. Cut two pieces of tan cardstock to 7 inches tall x 4½ inches wide. Cut two pieces of floral paper to 7 inches tall x 3½ inches wide. Cut one piece of ivory cardstock to 6 inches tall x 3½ inches wide. Fold the natural cardstock in half and score it with the bone folder to create a 7-inch-tall x 5-inch-wide card (it opens from the right).

2. Glue the two pieces of floral paper together (glue the white undersides together) to create double-sided floral paper.

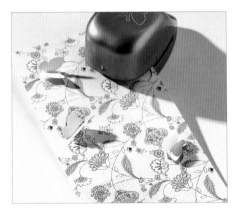

3. Punch butterflies in the floral paper using the butterfly lift punch.

NOTE: This tool punches half a butterfly and it will still be attached to the paper. After punching, carefully press the underside of the paper to push the butterfly wings up through the paper. Fold one wing to the left and one to the right to reveal a full butterfly. The butterfly will be white, as you are turning the inside of the paper out. The butterflies will then appear to "float" on top of the floral paper.

TIP: Tilt the punch at an angle to make the butterflies appear as if they're flying.

4. Apply glitter glue to each butterfly and allow to dry.

5. Once the butterflies are dry, center and adhere the floral paper to the tan cardstock.

6. Adhere the pink dotted ribbon to the edge of the floral paper where it meets the tan cardstock. Leave "tails" hanging off the edges of the card.

7. Tuck ribbon "tails" to the underside of the tan cardstock and glue down. Center and adhere the tan cardstock to the front of the card.

8. Transfer the "Daddy's Girl" rub-ons to the ivory cardstock using the popsicle stick. Center and adhere the ivory cardstock to the second piece of tan cardstock. Center and adhere the tan cardstock to the inside right of the card.

9. Adhere the Butterfly Kisses chipboard piece to the front of the card.

Angel Card

by WENDY WHITE

This is the perfect little card for the arrival of a new little angel here on earth.

SUPPLIES

Tools

- ☐ paper trimmer or cutting mat and knife
- ☐ ruler
- ☐ bone folder
- ☐ scissors

Materials

- ☐ lavender cardstock
- ☐ ivory cardstock
- ☐ floral paper
- ☐ purple ink pad
- ☐ adhesive

- ☐ definition of an angel (printed out from a computer using different fonts)
- ☐ purple-stitched ribbon (⅛ inch wide by 6 inches long)
- ☐ jump ring
- ☐ angel charm

INSTRUCTIONS

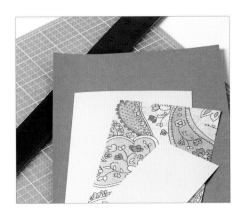

1. With the paper trimmer and ruler, measure and cut the lavender cardstock to 8½ inches tall x 5½ inches wide. Fold it in half and score with the bone folder to create a 4¼-inch-tall x 5½-inch-wide card (it opens from the bottom). Cut one piece of ivory cardstock to 3¾ inches tall x 5 inches wide (for the front matting) and a second piece of ivory cardstock to 2 inches tall x 3 inches wide (for the front center tag). Cut a third piece of ivory paper to 4 inches tall x 5 inches wide for the inside of the card. Cut the floral paper to 3¼ inches tall x 4½ inches wide. Ink edges of paper pieces with purple ink, if desired.

2. Center and adhere the floral paper to the 3¾-inch-tall x 5-inch-wide ivory cardstock. Adhere both to the front center of the card.

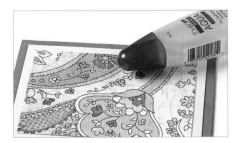

3. Adhere the angel definition to the ivory cardstock measuring 2 inches tall x 3 inches wide. Cut the purple ribbon to 6 inches. Run adhesive on the back of the ribbon and wrap it around the edge of the angel definition. Tie a small knot on the front near the bottom. Trim the ends of the ribbon.

4. Attach the angel tag to the front of the card, centered on the floral paper. Slide a jump ring through the angel charm and then slip it through the ribbon knot to hold it in place.

You Brighten My Days, Son

by RENÉE DEBLOIS

SUPPLIES

Tools

- ☐ paper trimmer or cutting mat and knife
- ☐ ruler
- ☐ die-cut machine and alphabet die cuts to spell "son"
- ☐ X-ACTO knife
- ☐ scissors

Materials

- ☐ red cardstock
- ☐ Dot Background stamp
- ☐ light blue stamp pad
- ☐ white cardstock
- ☐ Robot stamp
- ☐ black stamp pad
- ☐ adhesive
- ☐ blue note card
- ☐ dot ribbon
  (³⁄₈ inch wide x 8 inches long)
- ☐ tape
- ☐ foam mounting tape
- ☐ You Brighten My Days stamp

Let a robot show that you care with this very boy-friendly, everyday "I love you" card.

INSTRUCTIONS

1. With the paper trimmer and ruler, measure and cut the red cardstock to 2 1/4 inches x 2 1/4 inches square. Punch out the letters for "son" in red cardstock using the die-cut machine.

2. Stamp the Dot Background image in blue ink on the white cardstock. Stamp the Robot image over the dots in black ink. Cut out the image into a 2-inch x 2-inch square. Mat it onto the red cardstock square with adhesive.

3. Cut a 1/4-inch opening in the fold of the blue note card with the X-ACTO knife 2 inches from the bottom of the card. Feed the ribbon through the hole and bring both ends to meet at the front of the card. Trim ribbon as needed with scissors and tape the ends down. Line up the "son" letters 1/2 inch from the bottom and adhere them to the card.

4. Attach the robot and red cardstock square at an angle using foam mounting tape. Stamp "You Brighten My Days" in black ink at an angle above the tag.

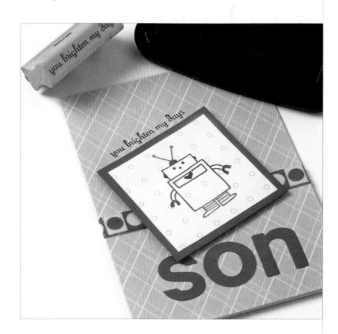

Li'l Love Bug

by SUSAN WEINROTH

Ladybugs are the loveliest of the bunch, and this hand-created bug is sure to please a little loved one.

SUPPLIES

Tools

- [ ] paper trimmer or cutting mat and knife
- [ ] ruler
- [ ] bone folder
- [ ] scissors
- [ ] circle cutter
- [ ] 1½-inch circle punch
- [ ] mini heart punch
- [ ] scallop-edged decorative scissors

Materials

- [ ] blue cardstock
- [ ] green cardstock
- [ ] adhesive
- [ ] white cardstock
- [ ] black cardstock
- [ ] red cardstock
- [ ] 2 silver brads
- [ ] black alphabet stickers
- [ ] red and white polka-dot ribbon (³⁄₈ inch wide by 6 inches long)

INSTRUCTIONS

1. With the paper trimmer and ruler, measure and cut the blue cardstock to 10 inches tall x 6 inches wide. Fold it in half and score with the bone folder to create a 5-inch-tall x 6-inch-wide card (it opens from the bottom).

2. Cut the green cardstock into a 1¾-inch-tall x 6-inch-wide strip. Use scissors to fringe-cut the top edge to simulate grass. Bend some "blades" forward. Adhere it to the bottom of the card.

3. Cut the white cardstock into circles and use scallop-edged scissors to cut edges to simulate clouds; adhere them to the top of the card.

4. Create the ladybug: Using the circle cutter, cut a 2-inch-tall x 4-inch-wide half-circle out of black cardstock. Cut the red cardstock slightly smaller and mat it to the black cardstock. Adhere it to the card, slipping it underneath the grass. With the 1½-inch circle punch, cut a 1½-inch circle out of black cardstock for the head and adhere it to the body. Cut two thin strips out of black cardstock for the antennae and adhere them to the head. Punch two small hearts out of red cardstock and glue them to the antennae. Punch nine hearts from the black cardstock and adhere them to body. Push the silver brads through for eyes.

5. Use the black alphabet stickers to spell "Li'l Love Bug" and adhere the words to the grass.

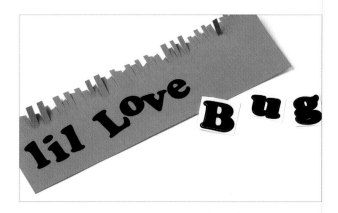

6. Adhere the red and white polka-dot ribbon below the greeting.

You Color My World

by KIMBERLY KESTI

Give your little loved ones something to keep them busy with this interactive card.

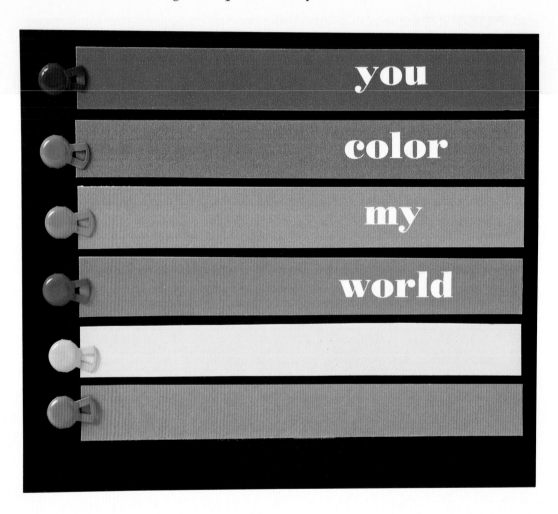

SUPPLIES

Tools

☐ paper trimmer or cutting mat and knife

☐ ruler

☐ bone folder

☐ computer with printer and word-processing software

☐ scissors

Materials

☐ white cardstock

☐ black cardstock

☐ brads in bright primary colors

☐ adhesive

☐ box of crayons

INSTRUCTIONS

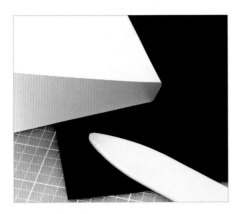

1. With the paper trimmer and ruler, measure and cut the white cardstock to 4 ¾ inches tall x 11½ inches wide. With the bone folder, score it at 5½ inches and 6 inches to create a box edge.

   Cut the black cardstock to 4¼ inches tall x 5 inches wide.

2. With the computer and printer, print strips of colored text boxes with white lettering. Trim the strips to ½ inch tall x 4½ inches wide. Attach each strip with a coordinating brad.

3. Print the inside message onto white cardstock and trim it with scissors to fit. Adhere the box of crayons inside the card.

4. Adhere black cardstock with colored strips to front of card.

CHAPTER 4

Cards for
Brothers and Sisters

If you have siblings, you know the special bond shared by brothers and sisters. Whether you were born just a few minutes apart or many years separate you, siblings provide a deep and binding relationship. This family bond cannot be broken regardless of geographic or even emotional distance.

Our siblings represent some of our longest-standing relationships. They are the people who have watched us grow and change over the years. They also know best which aspects of our personalities emerged as early as childhood. For better or worse, no one knows us more intimately than our brothers and sisters.

Sisters and brothers share secrets and gossip but also fight like cats and dogs. They help each other through tough times and are always available to celebrate the good times. Siblings can act as protective teammates or fierce adversaries. They can provide much-needed companionship or wise mentoring. The roller-coaster ride of emotions reflected in a sibling relationship is passionate and one of the strongest of human experiences.

Whether or not your sibling is a close friend, a handmade card speaks volumes and can be an unexpectedly moving gift. It can help you articulate your love in a way that can't be easily verbalized, as well as provide tangible proof of a family connectedness that transcends everyday life, roles, and responsibilities.

Sister Purse Box

by RENÉE DEBLOIS

This mini-handbag card holds a treasure trove of love and affection for a sister.

SUPPLIES

Tools

- [ ] sandpaper
- [ ] sponge brush
- [ ] pencil
- [ ] ruler
- [ ] paper trimmer or cutting mat and knife
- [ ] scissors
- [ ] white eraser
- [ ] scalloped oval punch
- [ ] ⅛-inch hole punch

- [ ] die-cut machine and/or alphabet die cuts
- [ ] T-pin, hammer
- [ ] wire cutters
- [ ] chain-nose pliers
- [ ] corner rounder

Materials

- [ ] mint tin
- [ ] primer
- [ ] glossy white spray paint
- [ ] three shades of white cardstock

- [ ] clear liquid glue
- [ ] mini glue dots
- [ ] spray adhesive
- [ ] glitter
- [ ] pop dots or foam mounting tape
- [ ] flat silver bead
- [ ] 24-gauge craft wire
- [ ] oval links silver chain (³⁄₈ inch wide by 10 inches long)
- [ ] photo
- [ ] alphabet stickers

INSTRUCTIONS

1. Clean the mint tin and sand it lightly with sandpaper. Paint one coat of primer with a sponge brush. When dry, spray the tin with glossy white spray paint. Allow to dry thoroughly.

2. With a pencil, trace the lid and bottom of the tin on one shade of white cardstock. Using a ruler, lightly draw diagonal lines ³⁄₄ inch from each other. Then draw 90-degree perpendicular lines ³⁄₄ inch from each other.

3. With the paper trimmer, cut strips of a second shade of white cardstock to ¹⁄₄ inch wide x about 5 inches long. Using clear liquid glue, adhere the strips over the drawn lines. Once dry, cut around the traced lines with scissors and erase any remaining pencil marks with a white eraser.

4. Adhere the top and bottom covers to the tin with mini glue dots.

5. Punch a scalloped oval from a third shade of white cardstock. Horizontally cut off the top third of the oval. Using a ¹⁄₈-inch hole punch, punch a hole into each individual scallop.

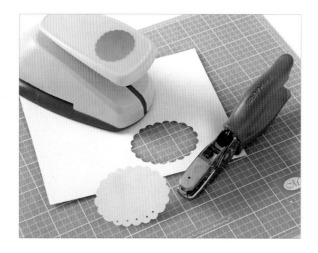

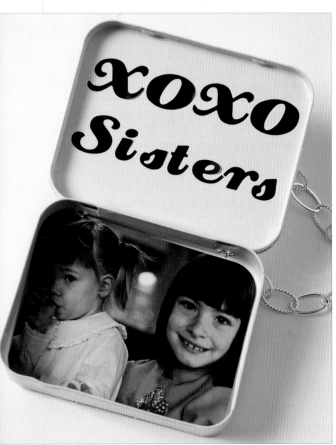

6. Using the die-cut machine, create the die-cut letters "sis" with the first shade of white cardstock.

7. Lightly spray the letters with a spray adhesive and sprinkle with fine glitter. Allow to dry.

8. Pick up the letters and glue them just below the flat part of the scalloped oval with clear liquid glue.

9. Affix the scallop to the tin with pop dots, aligning the flat top with the tin's edge.

10. Adhere a small silver bead to the scallop using a mini glue dot.

11. Create two tiny pairs of holes in the tin where the chain "strap" should begin and end. Do this by tapping lightly on a T-pin with a hammer.

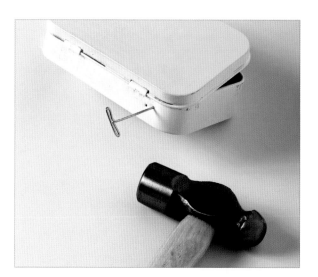

12. With wire cutters, cut two 2-inch pieces of 24-gauge craft wire. Bring together two ends of one piece of craft wire and catch an ending link of the silver chain in the loop. Feed each end of the craft wire through a hole and pull them inside the tin.

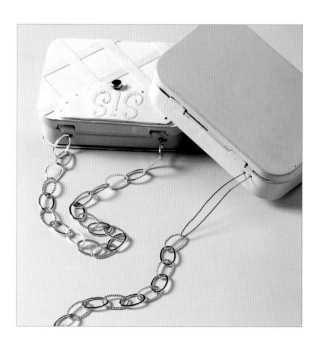

13. Tightly twist the wire inside the tin with chain-nose pliers and cut the excess wire. Repeat for the other side of the "strap."

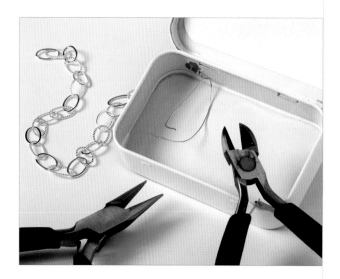

14. Cut a photo ¼ inch smaller all around than the bottom of the tin. Round the corners of the photo with the corner rounder. Adhere the photo to the interior bottom of the tin with mini glue dots.

15. Affix alphabet letter stickers to the inside lid of the tin.

Top 10 Reasons Why I Love You, Sis

by CANDICE CRUZ

SUPPLIES

Tools

☐ paper trimmer or cutting mat and knife

☐ ruler

☐ ¼-inch hole punch

Materials

☐ 12-inch square piece of patterned paper

☐ photo

☐ ten 4-inch square glassine envelopes with a flap

☐ satin ribbon (¼ inch wide by 14 inches long)

☐ alphabet rub-ons

☐ black journaling marker

You may have trouble deciding which 10 personality traits to highlight for this interactive pocket-pack of sisterly adoration.

INSTRUCTIONS

1. With the paper trimmer and ruler, cut the patterned paper into ten 3-inch x 3-inch squares. Crop the photo to a 3-inch x 3-inch square. Adhere one of the patterned paper squares to the back of the photo square.

2. Fold the flaps down on all of the envelopes. Stack nine of them on top of each other so that the flap is on the right side, facing up. Place the last envelope on top of the stack so that the flap is on the right side but facing down.

3. Use the 1/4-inch hole punch tool to make three holes along the left side of the stack of envelopes.

TIP: It may help to do two envelopes at a time.

4. Tie a 4 1/2-inch piece of ribbon through each hole and tie a loose double knot.

HINT: Don't make the knot too tight, or it will be difficult to turn each page.

5. Use rub-ons to number the flaps, create the cover title, and put a highlight on each piece of patterned paper.

6. Use a black journaling pen to write details on the back of each of the nine pieces of patterned paper. Slip the pieces into each of the glassine pockets. Insert the photo square backed on patterned paper into the first glassine envelope so the picture is the cover.

Brother

by WENDY WHITE

This elegant card in guy-friendly blue and tan provides a touch of class and affection.

Tools

- ☐ paper trimmer or cutting mat and knife
- ☐ ruler
- ☐ bone folder
- ☐ scallop-edged decorative scissors
- ☐ awl
- ☐ old mouse pad
- ☐ sewing machine
- ☐ popsicle stick

Materials

- ☐ brown cardstock
- ☐ coordinating patterned paper
- ☐ light brown solid paper
- ☐ light blue solid paper
- ☐ adhesive
- ☐ cream-colored thread
- ☐ white heart rub-ons or stickers
- ☐ brown alphabet rub-ons or stickers

INSTRUCTIONS

1. With the paper trimmer and ruler, measure and cut the brown cardstock to 8 1/2 inches tall x 5 1/4 inches wide. Fold it in half and score with the bone folder to make a 4 1/4-inch-tall x 5 1/4-inch wide card (it opens from the bottom). Trim the patterned paper to 3 1/2 inches tall x 5 1/2 inches wide (bottom layer); the light brown solid paper to 2 3/4 inches tall x 5 1/2 inches wide (second layer); the light blue solid paper to 2 inches tall x 5 1/2 inches wide (top layer); and the light blue solid paper to 4 1/4 inches tall x 5 1/2 inches wide (inside of card).

2. Use the scallop-edged scissors to trim the front bottom edge of the card. Use the awl, ruler, and mouse pad to punch holes in the scallops.

TIP: Be sure to punch from the front.

3. Adhere the light brown solid paper to the patterned paper. Then adhere the light blue paper to the top of the brown paper. Line up the edges and make sure all sides are equal and straight.

TIP: Do not adhere to the card yet.

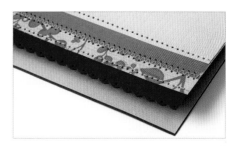

4. Machine stitch the papers using cream thread. Use a zigzag stitch to attach the light brown paper to the patterned paper and a straight stitch on the light blue and patterned papers. Adhere the assemblage to the front of the card.

5. Apply heart-shaped rub-ons or stickers to the center of the card using the popsicle stick. Layer the smaller heart on top of the larger heart. Apply rub-ons or stickers to spell "brother" over the hearts. Adhere the last piece of blue cardstock inside the card.

Red Sox

by RENÉE DEBLOIS

SUPPLIES

Tools

☐ paper trimmer or cutting mat and knife

☐ see-through ruler

☐ bone folder

☐ die-cut machine and pocket die cut

☐ popsicle stick

Materials

☐ natural cardstock

☐ two kinds of red and white striped paper

☐ navy blue cardstock

☐ adhesive tape runner

☐ rub-on letters

☐ game tickets

☐ sports team patch

TIP: Cardstock and patterned paper colors can be changed depending on team colors.

Tuck game tickets into this sports team-inspired card and you'll be favored forever.

INSTRUCTIONS

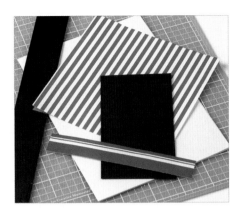

1. Using the paper trimmer and ruler, measure and cut the natural cardstock to 6 ¾ inches tall x 10 inches wide. Fold it in half and score with the bone folder to make a 6 ¾-inch-tall x 5-inch-wide card (it opens from the right). Cut the first kind of red and white striped paper into a rectangle 4 ⅞ inches tall x 5 inches wide. Cut the navy cardstock into a rectangle 2 ½ inches tall x 4 ½ inches wide. Cut the second kind of red and white striped paper into a strip ¾ inch tall x 5 inches wide.

2. Using the die-cut machine, punch out a pocket die-cut shape using navy cardstock. Adhere the pocket to the inside of the card.

NOTE: Do not apply glue to the top of the pocket.

3. Using the see-through ruler as a guide, center and apply the rub-on letters to the front of the card and the inside pocket using the popsicle stick. Insert the game tickets into the pocket.

4. On the front of the card, adhere the larger striped piece of paper to the bottom of the card. Adhere the navy cardstock to the top of the card and the smaller red and white striped paper over both to cover the seam. Attach the sports team patch to the card.

CHAPTER 5

Cards for Parents
and Grandparents

As we get older, we spend much of our time cultivating relationships with the people we have brought into our lives. Our spouses, children, and friends take center stage and demand our attention. Every so often, it is nice to turn our thoughts to those who came before us. Our parents and grandparents have showered us with so many gifts, words of love, and lessons over the years. A handmade card to celebrate their positive influence on our lives is always appreciated.

Special occasions such as Mother's Day, Father's Day, religious holidays, and birthdays provide a good opportunity to showcase our love for Mom and Dad with flowers or gifts. But a handmade card dropped in the mail is a welcome surprise for parents experiencing an empty nest or a lonely moment. Cards are also a great way to share simple news of daily life to feel more connected to parents with whom we may not speak every week. Take the time to write some details in your card. Mundane as they seem to you, these glimpses into your life will be of infinite interest to your mom and dad.

Grandparents are well known for spoiling grandchildren with treats, presents, and offers to bend the rules. We sometimes welcome their words of wisdom much more readily than those from our parents because of the difference in age and the more lighthearted relationship we share. If you are close to your grandmother and grandfather, show them you care with a happy little card that tells them they are special to you, too.

Grandma Card

by CANDICE CRUZ

SUPPLIES

Tools

- [ ] paper trimmer or cutting mat and knife
- [ ] see-through ruler
- [ ] bone folder
- [ ] awl
- [ ] old mouse pad
- [ ] pencil
- [ ] hand embroidery needle
- [ ] scissors
- [ ] computer with printer and word-processing software

Materials

- [ ] brown cardstock
- [ ] green and yellow embroidery floss
- [ ] tape
- [ ] yellow ribbon (¼-inch-wide by 3 feet long)
- [ ] red ribbon (¼-inch-wide by 1 foot long)
- [ ] mini glue dots
- [ ] brown seed beads
- [ ] dark yellow cardstock
- [ ] red cardstock

Grandma has loved and mentored you for years, so take the time to show her how much she means to you with this intricate card.

INSTRUCTIONS

1. Using the paper trimmer and ruler, measure and cut the brown cardstock to 8½ inches tall x 7 inches wide. Fold it in half and score with the bone folder to form a card 8½ inches tall x 3½ inches wide (it opens from the right). Tear off about ¼ inch along the right edge of the front of the card flap.

2. Open the card. On the left side, use an awl and an old mouse pad to punch holes in the shape of stems for the flowers.

TIP: It may be helpful to pencil in lines before making holes.

3. Thread the needle with green embroidery floss. Hand stitch the holes together. Tape any loose ends to the back of the card cover.

4. Cut the yellow ribbon into eighteen 1½-inch lengths. Adhere the ribbon ends to form petals. Use mini glue dots to adhere six petals together to form a flower.

5. Use the awl to punch a hole to the side of each petal in the center of the flower.

6. Thread the needle with yellow embroidery floss. Starting from behind the flower (the back of the card), come up through one of the holes. Thread four seed beads onto the needle. Insert the needle back down through a hole on the opposite side of the flower. Repeat until the center of the flower is complete with seed beads. Secure the end of the floss with a piece of tape on the back of the card.

7. Cut the red ribbon into six 1-inch pieces. To make each end into a V shape, fold the ribbon in half lengthwise and cut on a diagonal. Use mini glue dots to form a flower with four of the ribbon pieces.

8. Using the computer and printer, print the word "Grandma" and the message for the inside of the card onto the dark yellow cardstock. Use a ½-inch-tall x 2¼-inch-wide text box for "Grandma" and a 8¼-inch-tall x 2¼-inch-wide text box for the inside message.

9. Cut the word "Grandma" into a ½-inch-tall x 2¼-inch-wide rectangle. Mat it onto a piece of red cardstock that is ¾ inch tall x 2½ inches wide. Cut the inside message into a 8½-inch-tall x 2¼-inch-wide rectangle. Mat it onto a piece of red cardstock that is 8¾ inches tall x 2½ inches wide. Hand embroider around the edges of the yellow cardstock pieces. Adhere "Grandma" on the outside of the card and the message on the inside.

10. Cut a 8¼-inch-tall x 3-inch-wide rectangle out of brown cardstock to adhere to the left side of the inside of the card to cover up the taped pieces of embroidery floss.

To the Best Grandpa

by CANDICE CRUZ

Grandpa will be impressed by your creativity and appreciate your loving words with this card.

to the best GRANDPA in the world

SUPPLIES

Tools

- [ ] paper trimmer or cutting mat and knife
- [ ] ruler
- [ ] bone folder
- [ ] X-ACTO knife
- [ ] pencil
- [ ] die-cut machine and leaf die cut
- [ ] ⅛-inch hole punch
- [ ] eyelet-setting tool and hammer
- [ ] scissors

Materials

- [ ] white cardstock
- [ ] glittery dark red paper
- [ ] adhesive
- [ ] copper metal paper
- [ ] six ⅛-inch copper eyelets
- [ ] hemp cord
- [ ] brown marker

INSTRUCTIONS

1. With the paper trimmer and ruler, measure and cut the white cardstock to 10 inches tall x 7 inches wide. Fold it in half and score with the bone folder to form a 5-inch-tall x 7-inch-wide card (it opens from the bottom). Cut the dark red paper into a 3-inch-tall x 6-inch-wide rectangle. Tear along the edges about ¼ inch.

2. Center and adhere the red rectangle on the front of the card. Open the card. Use an X-ACTO knife to cut out a 2-inch-tall x 5-inch-wide rectangle in the center of the dark red paper, going through the white cardstock as well.

TIP: Use a ruler and lightly pencil where you will cut.

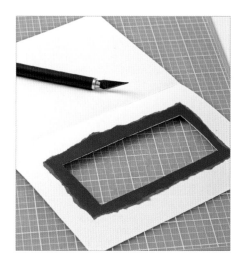

3. Using the die-cut machine, cut three leaves from the copper metal paper. Punch a hole in each leaf and set a copper eyelet with the eyelet-setting tool and hammer. Punch three holes along the top of the dark red frame. Set a copper eyelet in each hole.

4. With scissors, cut the hemp cord into three 6-inch-long pieces. Tie a knot at the end of one piece and thread it through the top of a leaf. Thread the other end through an eyelet on the dark red frame. Tie another knot to secure it in place and then trim the end. Repeat with the two other leaves.

5. Use a marker to write a message along the bottom right corner under the dark red frame.

Dad, My Hero

by RENÉE DEBLOIS

SUPPLIES

Tools

- ☐ square scalloped punch
- ☐ pencil
- ☐ white eraser
- ☐ die-cut machine and library-plate die
- ☐ ⅛-inch hole punch
- ☐ paper trimmer or cutting mat and knife
- ☐ ruler

Materials

- ☐ dark brown note card
- ☐ Watermark stamp pad
- ☐ Man of the Year stamp
- ☐ Superhero stamp
- ☐ black stamp pad
- ☐ brown, flesh-colored, and aqua markers
- ☐ blue-striped ribbon (⅝ inch wide by 9 inches long)
- ☐ tape
- ☐ aqua cardstock
- ☐ brown brads
- ☐ white cardstock
- ☐ Dad stamp
- ☐ My Hero stamp
- ☐ foam mounting tape
- ☐ liquid glue

Show Dad he's your everyday hero when he offers his common-sense advice, his help with car trouble, or a few needed bucks.

INSTRUCTIONS

1. Situate the note card so that the fold is at the top. Using the Watermark stamp pad, stamp "Man of the Year" at equal intervals three times across and three times down the note card.

2. Punch a square scalloped "window" out of the top right corner, leaving ½ inch from the right edge of the card.

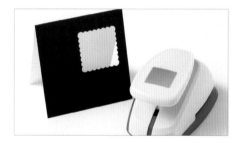

3. Lightly draw pencil marks inside the card at the four corners of the scallop to indicate where the Superhero image should go. Open the card and stamp the Superhero within the marks with the black stamp pad. Erase the pencil marks.

4. Color in the Superhero and his costume with markers. Draw a "D" on his chest with the brown marker. Stamp "Happy Father's Day" inside the card.

5. Wrap the blue-striped ribbon around the card, aligning the bottom edge ¼ inch from the bottom of the card. Bring the ribbon ends to meet at the front of the card and tape the ends down.

6. Using the die-cut machine, cut out the library plate die cut from the aqua cardstock. Align the library plate with the ribbon and punch ⅛-inch holes through the card and ribbon using the die plate holes as a guide. Affix the library plate to the card using brown brads.

7. Using the paper trimmer and ruler, cut a piece of white cardstock to ¾ inch tall x 2½ inches wide. Stamp "Dad" horizontally and "My Hero" vertically. Attach to the library plate using a strip of foam mounting tape to add dimension.

For You, Mom, with Love

by CANDICE CRUZ

SUPPLIES

Tools

☐ paper trimmer or cutting mat and knife

☐ ruler

☐ large flower punch

☐ small flower punch

☐ bone folder

☐ pencil

☐ scissors

☐ corner rounder

☐ popsicle stick

Materials

☐ dark brown cardstock

☐ red paper

☐ glue pen

☐ glue dots

☐ flat-backed rhinestones

☐ foam mounting tape

☐ white alphabet rub-ons or stickers

☐ fine-tip black marker

☐ peach ribbon (¼ inch wide by 18 inches long)

☐ safety pin

Flowers and sparkly things are a girl's best friend, so Mom will know just how much you care when you give her a card adorned with dozens of handmade paper flowers and rhinestones.

INSTRUCTIONS

1. With the paper trimmer and ruler, measure and cut the dark brown cardstock to 6 inches tall x 12 inches wide. Cut the red paper into a 5-inch-tall x 5-inch-wide square (for the inside of the card). Cut another piece of red paper into a 1½-inch-tall x 3-inch-wide rectangle (for the tag). Use more red paper to punch 40 large flowers (with the big flower punch) and 13 small flowers (with the small flower punch).

2. Fold the edges of the dark brown cardstock inward to create a gatefold (with 3-inch flaps on each side). Score with the bone folder.

3. Lightly pencil a heart shape on the front of the card. Use a drop of liquid glue from the glue pen to adhere each of the larger flowers to the card, creating a heart shape (be sure to overlap the flowers a little).

Tip: Cut the flowers in half with scissors before adhering them where the flaps open.

4. Use the mini glue dots to adhere the rhinestones to the centers of each smaller flower. Use a small piece of foam mounting tape to adhere the smaller flowers in a scattered pattern on the heart. The foam mounting tape will make the smaller flowers "pop up."

5. Use the corner rounder to round the corners of the small rectangular tag.

6. Use popsicle stick to transfer the white alphabet rub-ons or stickers to spell "Mom" in the center of the tag.

7. Use a black marker to handwrite "for you" and "with love" above and below "Mom."

8. Open the card and glue the red paper square to the inside center of the card.

9. Close the card. Tie the ribbon into a double knot or a bow around the card. Cut the ends of the ribbon at an angle.

10. Thread a safety pin through the small tag and then through the tied ribbon.

CHAPTER 6

Cards for Friends

Friends sprinkle fun into our lives. Unlike our family, we get to choose our friends. They are a reflection of who we are and who we aspire to be. With our friends, we get to experience, discuss, and enjoy all aspects of our lives. When we have a bad day, a friend is the first person we call. When we get great news, a friend is the one we rush to tell.

Friends make us laugh. In the summer, they kidnap us and take us on joyrides with the windows rolled down and the music turned up high. In the winter, we share a cup of hot cocoa and dish gossip in a cozy neighborhood café. When we're sad, they take us shopping. And when we're happy, they are happy for us.

Everyone with good friends knows that in order to have close friendships, we must first learn to be good friends ourselves. We must never take friendships for granted. It is essential to nurture friendships so that they can grow over the years. The time and energy we put into our friendships reaps incredible rewards for decades to come. Choose one or more of the handmade cards here and put your friend in the limelight— something he or she does for you all the time.

You Bring Out the Best in Me

by CANDICE CRUZ

Tell a special friend he or she is helping you achieve your dreams with this sweet card.

SUPPLIES

Tools

- [ ] outline letter stamps
- [ ] computer with printer and word-processing program
- [ ] cutting mat and knife
- [ ] ruler
- [ ] ¼-inch hole punch
- [ ] eyelet-setting tool and hammer
- [ ] heart punch

Materials

- [ ] black ink pad
- [ ] 3¼-inch green scalloped square
- [ ] adhesive
- [ ] 4¼-inch square blue note card
- [ ] white cardstock
- [ ] 2 silver eyelets
- [ ] satin ribbon (¼ inch wide by 9 inches long)
- [ ] red cardstock

INSTRUCTIONS

1. Using the outline letter stamps and black ink pad, stamp the words "you" and "me" onto the green scalloped square, making sure you leave room in the middle for the white piece of cardstock.

2. Adhere the scalloped square to the center of the note card.

3. Using a computer and printer, print out "bring out the best in" onto white cardstock. Use the cutting mat, knife, and ruler to cut out the phrase, leaving about ½ inch on each side.

4. Adhere the white strip of cardstock to the scalloped square in between "you" and "me."

5. Use the hole punch to make a hole on either side of the white strip of cardstock.

6. Set two eyelets with the eyelet-setting tool and hammer.

7. Attach the ribbon, weaving the ribbon into the first eyelet (left side) underneath the sentiment and coming back out of the second eyelet. Tie a double knot on the front of the card. Cut the ribbon on a diagonal at the ends.

8. Punch out a heart from the piece of red cardstock and adhere it in the middle of the "o" in "you."

Heartfelt Wishes

by CANDICE CRUZ

Friendships grow roots with heartfelt wishes from the tree of love in this shiny little card.

SUPPLIES

Tools

☐ large scalloped square paper punch and scissors

Materials

☐ Leafy Tree stamp

☐ brown ink pad

☐ white cardstock

☐ green marker

☐ 5 small heart sequin stickers

☐ fine-tip black marker

☐ 4¼-inch green square note card

☐ tape

☐ dots ribbon (⅜ inch wide by 9 inches long)

☐ foam mounting tape

☐ Heartfelt Wishes stamp

INSTRUCTIONS

1. Stamp the Leafy Tree image in brown ink onto a piece of white cardstock. Allow the ink to dry.

2. Center the image in the large scalloped square punch tool and punch out.

3. Color in the leaves with a green marker.

4. Place the heart sequin stickers at random levels under the branches of the stamped tree image.

5. With a fine-tip black marker, draw a line from the top of each heart sticker to a tree branch; draw in two ribbon bows on the branch to make it look like a knot.

6. Hold the note card base so that the closed edge is at the top of the card.

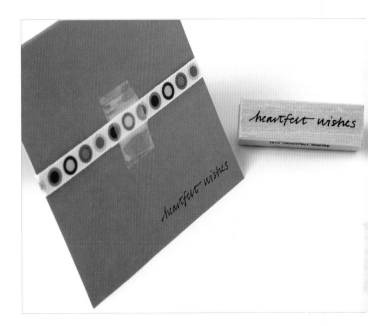

7. Tape one end of the ribbon to the center of the card front. Wrap it around and tape the other end to secure it in place. Trim off any excess with scissors.

8. Place a piece of foam mounting tape on the back of the white cardstock scallop and center it onto the front of the card. Press down to secure it in place.

9. Stamp Heartfelt Wishes in the bottom right corner of the card.

You Make My World Brighter

by SUSAN WEINROTH

SUPPLIES

Tools

- [ ] paper trimmer or cutting mat and knife
- [ ] ruler
- [ ] bone folder
- [ ] corner rounder
- [ ] circle cutter
- [ ] computer with printer and word-processing software
- [ ] scissors
- [ ] sewing machine

Materials

- [ ] yellow cardstock
- [ ] orange patterned paper
- [ ] adhesive
- [ ] yellow patterned paper
- [ ] variety of ribbons in coordinating colors (¼ inch to ⅝ inch wide by 2 inches long)
- [ ] yellow thread
- [ ] yellow flat-backed rhinestones

Rays of sunshine shout out love and happiness in this colorful card.

INSTRUCTIONS

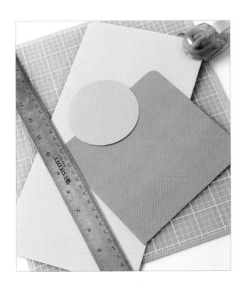

1. With the paper trimmer and ruler, measure and cut the yellow cardstock to 6 inches tall x 12 inches wide. Fold it in half and score with the bone folder to make a 6-inch x 6-inch square card (it opens from the right). Cut a 6-inch x 6-inch piece of orange patterned paper. Adhere the orange paper to the front of the card. Use the corner rounder to round all four corners. Cut a 3½-inch-diameter circle from the yellow patterned paper to use as a sun.

2. Cut 1½-inch-long pieces of various ribbons. Adhere them underneath the sun. Adhere the sun with rays to the front of the card.

3. Using the computer and printer, print out the greeting onto the yellow cardstock. Cut into individual words with scissors and glue them to the body of the sun.

4. Machine sew (straight stitch) around the edges of sun using yellow thread.

5. Adhere the yellow rhinestones around the circumference of the sun.

Love and Chocolate

by CANDICE CRUZ

Mmm ... chocolate! Be sure to send a sweet little treat along with this sweet note.

all a girl really needs is LOVE

... but a little CHOCOLATE now and then sure doesn't hurt!

SUPPLIES

Tools

- [ ] paper trimmer or cutting mat and knife
- [ ] computer with printer and word-processing software
- [ ] bone folder
- [ ] scallop-edged decorative scissors
- [ ] scissors
- [ ] 1¼-inch circle punch

Materials

- [ ] cream cardstock
- [ ] adhesive
- [ ] green satin ribbon (1½ inches wide by 8½ inches long)
- [ ] brown cardstock
- [ ] vellum
- [ ] tape
- [ ] iridescent white fabric paint
- [ ] mini glue dots

INSTRUCTIONS

1. With the paper trimmer and ruler, measure and cut a piece of cream cardstock to 8 ½ inches tall x 11 inches wide. With the computer and printer, print the wording onto the cardstock, leaving a 2-inch space between the top and bottom of the text boxes.

2. Cut the cream cardstock to form an 8-inch-tall x 8 ½-inch-wide rectangle. Fold it in half and score with the bone folder to form a 4-inch-tall x 8 ½-inch-wide card (it opens from the bottom).

3. Use the scallop-edged scissors to cut about ¼ inch from the bottom of the card front.

4. Adhere the ribbon to the card between the text and trim the edges flush with scissors.

5. Using the circle punch, punch five 1 ¼-inch circles out of brown cardstock. Trim ⅛ inch off the bottom of each.

6. Cut the vellum into five 1 ¾-inch-tall x 2-inch-wide rectangles. Hold each vellum piece so that it is horizontal, then use the scallop-edged scissors to trim about ⅛ inch off the top.

7. Fold each vellum piece in half lengthwise with the scalloped edge on top. Fold each side toward the back and in a diagonal. Secure on the back with a piece of tape.

8. Place a brown circle inside each vellum cup.

9. Squiggle white fabric paint to accent the top of each chocolate.

10. Adhere the chocolates on top of the ribbon with mini glue dots.

Who I Love

by CANDICE CRUZ

SUPPLIES

Tools

☐ pencil

☐ scissors

☐ paper trimmer or cutting mat and knife

☐ ruler

☐ corner rounder

☐ label maker

☐ ¼-inch hole punch

Materials

☐ clean mint tin

☐ orange, green, and blue double-sided patterned paper

☐ adhesive

☐ black marker

☐ large green alphabet stickers

☐ small brown alphabet stickers

☐ yellow ribbon (¼ inch wide by 2 feet long)

☐ photographs

☐ fine-tip marker

Give a friend this pocket-sized mini book of her favorite people to carry around and remember who loves her.

INSTRUCTIONS

1. With a pencil, trace the bottom of the mint tin on the back of the patterned paper four times. Cut out with scissors. Adhere the patterned paper to the top and bottom of the tin, then on the inside of the tin under the lid and along the bottom.

2. With the paper trimmer and ruler, measure and cut a piece of patterned paper into a ⅝-inch-tall x 12-inch-wide strip. Adhere this paper to the walls of the inside of the tin. Cut a piece of patterned paper into a ½-inch-tall x 12-inch-wide strip. Adhere this to the outside edge of the tin. Make sure the edge is flush with the bottom of the tin so that the lid can close.

3. Use a black marker to make dashed lines along the edges of the larger letters, spelling "who." Use the small alphabet stickers to spell "I love." Adhere to the front of the tin.

TIP: Work from the right to left, spelling "I love" back-ward, so the "e" will be along the right edge of the tin.

4. Adhere the ribbon above the word "who" and trim to fit. Adhere ribbon next to "I love." Trim the left edge at an angle and the right edge flat. Adhere a piece of ribbon around the edge of the lid.

5. For the inside pages, trim photos to 2 inches tall x 1¾ inches wide. Cut patterned paper into 3¼-inch-tall x 2-inch-wide rectangles to mat each photo. Adhere a photo to each rectangle, leaving an ⅛-inch margin on the left, top, and right sides of the photo. Use small alphabet stickers to spell out the person's name below the photo. Round the corners of the rectangles.

6. Use a label maker to spell out the person's relation-ship to you below his or her name. Punch a hole in the bottom right corner of each rectangle. With a fine-tip marker, write bits of information about each person on the back of the rectangles, such as date of birth and things that you love about him or her. Tie all the rectangles together with a piece of ribbon and place inside the tin.

CHAPTER 7

Expressions of Love

GREETINGS

Choosing a greeting or sentiment for your card is an important first step in setting the right tone. First decide which type of card style you want—be it classic, modern, humorous, cute, intricate, or some other style. Your greeting and message will often dictate the types of materials you use, the layout of your card, the images you will incorporate, and any unique features or embellishments you will add. Greetings and sentiments can be handmade using a computer and printer. They can be created with rubber stamps and ink. You can also find stickers, rub-ons, and other embellishments to do the trick for you.

QUOTATIONS

There's nothing wrong with stealing the words out of someone else's mouth if they fit what you're trying to say. Quotations can simply and succinctly convey your feelings to your loved ones. The Web sites www.coolquotes.com and www.worldofquotes.com are helpful resources for quotations.

HANDWRITING

In today's technology-driven world, there's nothing sexier and more intimate than personal handwriting. Take the time to handwrite your message for a truly personal approach. If you don't like the look of your own handwriting, incorporate just a bit of it into your card. You can sign your name yourself or write your loved one's name or initials. Use a computer, rubber stamps, or rub-ons for the rest of your text.

POSTAL REGULATIONS

Cards of unique shapes, sizes, and weights may require special postage to mail. Always check with your local post office for proper postage to ensure your handmade card arrives at your loved one's home. Also, try not to mail your card on days when there is inclement weather to avoid smudging and water damage.

CHAPTER 8

Resources

DETAILED SUPPLY LISTS

Each handmade card featured in *Love Notes* was created using a variety of tools and materials. Below are detailed supply lists for each card to find specific materials to replicate the cards found in this book.

You Complete Me by Wendy White

Bazzill Basics Paper: Wild Pansy and Vanilla cardstock

KI Memories: Frosty alphabet-patterned paper

Making Memories: Love hot pink rub-ons

Flying High Up on the Wings of Love
by Kimberly Kesti

Bazzill Basics Paper: KI Green Tea, KI Black and White cardstock

Dafont: Attic Antique font

Hambly Screen Prints: Wings rub-ons

Me and My Big Ideas: Chester and Juniper patterned paper

Love Grows by Wendy White

Bazzill Basics Paper: KI White cardstock in Orange Peel, Canvas, and Smooth textures

Carolee's Creations: Red LOVE stickers

Fontwerks: Fresh Foliage Baby's Breath stamp

Where I Go by Wendy White

Bazzill Basics Paper: Kraft, Pear, and Pomegranate cardstock

Emagination: Heart punch

Li'l Davis Designs: Map-patterned paper

Scrapsupply: SP You've Got Mail and SP Sweetie Pie fonts

Your Love Brings Color to My World
by Susan Weinroth

American Crafts: Brown ribbon

Bazzill Basics Paper: Amaretto and Brown Bling cardstock

Fabri-Tac: Fabric glue

Fiskars: Pinking shears

Fontwerks: Patterned paper

May Arts: Tan ribbon

Two Peas in a Bucket: Typo font

Westrim Crafts: Rhinestones

Love Potion #9 by Renée DeBlois

A Muse Art Stamps: Pink Mod Dot note card, Love Potion #9 stamp, Boris/Mad Scientist stamp, Brewing Up Some Fun stamp

Bazzill Basics Paper: Criss Cross Candy Apple and White cardstock

Offray: Black and white ribbon

With U I Can Just Be Me by Candice Cruz

A Muse Art Stamps: To/From/Parentheses stamp

Bazzill Basics Paper: Bazzill White, Cheddar, Chiffon, Ivy, Jetstream, Lakeshore, and Bahama cardstock

EK Success: Primitive Heart punch

Fontwerks: George Outline Large U stamp

PSX: Antique Alphabet stamps

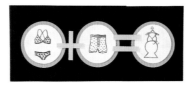

Oh Baby! by Candice Cruz

A Muse Art Stamps: Lingerie, Boy Shorts, and Maternity Dress stamps

Creative Memories: Circle cutting tool

Die Cuts with a View: Black, horizontal gate-closed card

EK Success: Zig 2-way glue pen

Paper Source: Chartreuse cardstock

Savvy Stamps: Oh Baby! stamp

Stampendous: Multi ultrafine crystal glitter

In Love There Is No Measure of Time
by Kimberly Kesti

Bazzill Basics Paper: Bubblegum and White cardstock

Creative Imaginations: Narratives, Antique Medley Collection, White Line Scalloped paper

Daisy D's: The Girlfriend Collection, Girlfriend Stripe, Passion Pink patterned paper

Doodlebug: Tokens, Red Hearts accent

Heidi Swapp: Clocks, Jet Paper, Bling, Frames, Jems

May Arts: Ribbon

Microsoft Word: CK Academia and English Vivace fonts

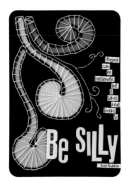

Be Silly by Candice Cruz

Bazzill Basics Paper: Bazzill White, Black Tie Bling, Blue Eyes Bling, Bright Lights Bling, and Envy Bling cardstock

Heidi Swapp: Center of Attention white chipboard letters

Scrapsupply: SP Wonderful Wendy (sizes 14 and 10) font

You Have My Heart Tied Up with Love
by Kimberly Kesti

Bazzill Basics Paper: Light Sky cardstock

Blue Cardigan Designs: Imagination Project, Evana's Hearts patterned paper

May Arts: Red gingham ribbon

Happy 5th Anniversary
by Renée DeBlois

3M: Inkjet transparency

American Crafts: Black brads

Bazzill Basics Paper: Natural cardstock

Coats & Clark: Thread

Creating Keepsakes: Birthright font

Glue Dots: Mini glue dots

K&Company: Premade 5-inch x 7-inch tag card

Microsoft Word: Baskerville Old Face font

Ranger: Pop It Dots dimensional dot adhesive

Waverly: Rustic Life Resort Garnet toile fabric

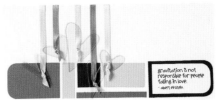

Gravitation Is Not Responsible
by Candice Cruz

Bazzill Basics Paper: Bazzill White, Jetstream, Lakeshore, and Bahama cardstock

Heidi Swapp: Ghost Shapes clear plastic hearts

Paper Source: Butter and Poppy ribbon

Scrapsupply: SP Toggle font

Hot Stuff by Susan Weinroth

American Crafts: Black ribbon

Bazzill Basics Paper: Bazzill Pink cardstock

Bo Bunny: Zebra-patterned paper

Glue Dots: Pop dots

KI Memories: Pink Print, Black Stripe patterned paper

Making Memories: Square medium tag rim

Two Peas in a Bucket: Typo font

True Love by Kimberly Kesti

Bazzill Basics Paper: KI Black and Lily White cardstock

Mod: Blackbird Stripe paper

Stampin' Up: Love stamp

Color Box: Chalk ink, lavender

Hero Arts: Clear embossing powder

Karen Foster: Jeweled brad

Making Memories: True tag

Love by Kimberly Kesti

7 Gypsies: Printed twill ribbon

Autumn Leaves: Foofala Red, Black and Cream Collection patterned paper

Bazzill Basics Paper: Old Flame, Dark Sand, and Black cardstock

EK Success: Nostalgiques Collection key

Fontwerks: Bohemina Rhapsody stamps

Hero Arts: Clear embossing powder

Tsukineko: StazOn black ink

I'm Smitten by Renée DeBlois

American Crafts: Bookshelf Bradbury, Snicket, and Grimm patterned papers; Keswick ribbon; Remarks hickory brown letter stickers; brown brads

Ellison: Big Shot die-cut machine and mitten die cuts

Glue Dots: Mini glue dots

Manos del Uruguay: Yarn

Woody Allen Quotation by Candice Cruz

Bazzill Basics Paper: Bottle Glass and Applesauce cardstock

Chatterbox: Soft Flowering Vine patterned paper

Junkitz: Mom long brads

Posh Impressions: Primitive Heart punch

Myfonts.com: Montreal (size 16) font

XOXO by Candice Cruz

American Crafts: Ribbons #88411 (red), #88386 (dots on white background), #88387 (striped), #88355 (dots on red background)

Bazzill Basics Paper: Pink Cadillac Bling and Cream cardstock

Posh Impressions: Heart punch

Savvy Stamps: XOXO stamp

To-Do List by Wendy White

7 Gypsies: Family Profile patterned paper

American Crafts: Downtown Orange #1 ribbon

Bazzill Basics Paper: Dark Tangerine cardstock

Urban Lily: Be Yourself, Be Strong striped paper

The Heart Has Its Reasons by Renée DeBlois

3M: Super 77 spray adhesive

Bazzill Basics Paper: White and Ruby Slipper cardstock

Hewlett-Packard: Photo paper

Microsoft Word: Century Gothic font

Happy Birthday by Renée DeBlois

Anna Griffin: Happy and Birthday stamps

Bazzill Basics Paper: White, Parakeet, and Petunia cardstock

DMC: Hot pink embroidery floss

Making Memories: Pink mailbox tile "O," pink flower embellishment

Malabrigo: Sapphire yarn

Paper Salon: Outline Flower stamp

Scenic Route Paper Co.: Capitol Hill Clover chipboard "X"

Scrapworks: Monterey Bloom paper

Butterfly Kisses by Wendy White

Bazzill Basics Paper: Amaretto and Travertine cardstock

Basic Grey: Lily Kate Parasol paper

EK Success: Medium Butterfly Lift Paper Shapers punch

K&Company: Butterfly Kisses Chipboard To Go

Offray: Pink with white dots ribbon

Ranger Ink: Crystal Ice Stickles Glitter Glue

Angel Card by Wendy White

A Charming Place: Angel charm

Basic Grey: Lily Kate Wisteria patterned paper

Bazzill Basics Paper: Purple cardstock

Making Memories: Angel definition sticker

You Brighten My Days, Son
by Renée DeBlois

American Crafts: Windsor Dot ribbon

A Muse Art Stamps: You Brighten My Days stamp

Bazzill Basics Paper: Criss Cross Candy Apple and Bazzill White cardstock

Ellison: Big Shot die-cut machine and Block Party alphabet die cuts

Savvy Stamps: Premade blue note card, Large Outline Dot Background stamp, Valentine Robot stamp

Li'l Love Bug by Susan Weinroth

American Crafts: Matte silver brads, red polka-dot ribbon, Charlie Jr. black stickers

Bazzill Basics Paper: Snow Cone, Tomato, Raven, White, and Worldwin Grass Green cardstock

EK Success: Mini heart punch

Fiskars: Cloud decorative scissors, circle cutter

You Color My World by Kimberly Kesti

Bazzill Basics Paper: Black and White cardstock

Karen Foster: Loopy Brads, Brights and Primary

Microsoft Word: Poster Bodoni font

Sister Purse Box by Renée DeBlois

American Crafts: Alphabet stickers

Bazzill Basics Paper: White cardstock

Glitterex: Ultra Fine Crystal Clear glitter

Glue Dots: Mini glue dots

Kilz: Primer

Ranger: Pop-It Dots dimensional adhesive

Rust-Oleum Lacquer: Gloss White spray paint

Top 10 Reasons Why I Love You, Sis
by Candice Cruz

American Crafts: Jack Jr. black alphabet rub-ons, Jack Jr. Sidekicks black rub-ons, Ned Jr. red mini marks rub-ons, Pigment Pro black marker (tip size .03)

Chatterbox: Scrapbook Walls, Light Orchard Blossom, double-sided patterned paper

Paper Source: Glassine envelopes, Papaya ribbon

Brother by Wendy White

Basic Grey: Heart rub-ons

Bazzill Basics Paper: Hershey cardstock

Chatterbox: Dorm Sky Campus Flower patterned paper

Crate Paper: Brother rub-ons

Red Sox by Renée DeBlois

Bazzill Basics Paper: White and Navy cardstock

EK Success: Red Sox patch

Making Memories: Heidi large white rub-ons

Paper Source: Red and white striped paper

Grandma Card
by Candice Cruz

American Crafts: Yellow and red ribbon

Bazzill Basics Paper: Nutmeg and Pomegranate cardstock

DMC: Embroidery floss 166 and 725

Scrapsupply: SP Chicken Noodle (size 20) and SP Inspired (size 48) fonts

To the Best Grandpa
by Candice Cruz

ArtEmboss: Copper lightweight metal paper

Ellison: Big Shot die-cut machine and Leaf #3 die cut

Paper Source: Mars Stardream paper

Dad, My Hero by Renée DeBlois

3M: Adhesive foam mounting tape

American Crafts: Brown brads

A Muse Art Stamps: Premade French Roast square note card, Hero stamp, Dad stamp, My Hero stamp

Bazzill Basics Paper: Swimming Pool and White cardstock

Ellison: Big Shot die-cut machine and Library Plate die cut

Inkadinkado: Man of the Year stamp

Marvy Uchida: Le Plume II markers, Aquamarine #74, Pale Pink #47, and Dark Brown #18

Tsukineko: Versamark Watermark stamp pad

For You, Mom, with Love by Candice Cruz

3M: Adhesive foam mounting tape
American Crafts: Pigment Pro marker (size .03 tip)

Bazzill Basics Paper: Espresso cardstock

EK Success: ZIG chisel-tip glue pen

Glue Dots: Mini glue dots

Making Memories: Heidi Lowercase black alphabet rub-ons

Marvy Uchida: Flower paper punch

Paper Source: Strawberry and Poppy paper, Poppy ribbon

You Bring Out the Best in Me by Candice Cruz

A Muse Art Stamps: French Blue Solid note card

Fontwerks: George Outline stamps

Paper Source: Chartreuse Scalloped Square card, Poppy ribbon

Heartfelt Wishes by Candice Cruz

American Crafts: Ribbon #88295, Leaf Memory marker, Pigment Pro black marker (tip size .03)

A Muse Art Stamps: Fern Solid note card; Leafy Tree stamp; Creative Candy Mini Heart twinkle stickers

Marvy Uchida: Giga Scallop Square punch

Savvy Stamps: Heartfelt Wishes stamp

You Make My World Brighter by Susan Weinroth

American Crafts: Premium Elements Ribbon

Bazzill Basics Paper: Yellow and Yellow Bling cardstock

KI Memories: Yellow patterned paper

May Arts: Ribbon

Pebbles: Ribbon

Scrapworks: Orange patterned paper

Two Peas in a Bucket: Typo font
Westrim Crafts: Rhinestones

Love and Chocolate by Candice Cruz

Bazzill Basics Paper: Sugar Daddy Bling cardstock

Dafont: Chocolate Box (size 60) fonts

EK Success: 1 ¼-inch circle punch tool

Fiskars: Paper Edgers Scallop scissors

Paper Source: Rhubarb and Chartreuse paper

Tulip: Matte Snow Cap White dimensional fabric paint

TypeNow: Seraphic Organism (size 18)

Who I Love by Candice Cruz

American Crafts: Pigment Pro black marker (size .03 tip)

Dymo: Label Buddy label maker

Making Memories: Meadow Chunky Creative Letters and Brown Little Letters Chunky Style alphabet stickers

Paper Source: Butter ribbon

My Mind's Eye: Wild Asparagus Orange/Blue Polka Dot and Blue/Orange Stripe double-sided cardstock

SUPPLIERS

The handmade cards that appear in *Love Notes* were created using products from a variety of suppliers. Please visit the manufacturers' Web sites below for more information about specific products and to locate craft stores near you that carry these products.

3M: www.3m.com

7 Gypsies: www.sevengypsies.com

A Charming Place: www.acharmingplace.com

American Crafts: www.americancrafts.com

A Muse Art Stamps: www.amuseartstamps.com

Anna Griffin: www.annagriffin.com

Autumn Leaves: www.autumnleaves.com

Basic Grey: www.basicgrey.com

Bazzill Basics Paper: www.bazzillbasics.com

Beacon Adhesives (Fabri-Tac): www.beaconcreates.com

Bo Bunny: www.bobunny.com

Carolee's Creations: www.adornit.com

Chatterbox: www.chatterboxinc.com

Coats & Clark: www.coatsandclark.com

ColorBox: www.clearsnap.com

Crate Paper: www.cratepaper.com

Creating Keepsakes: www.creatingkeepsakes.com

Creative Imaginations: www.creativeimaginations.us

Creative Memories: www.creativememories.com

Dafont: www.dafont.com

Daisy D's: www.daisyds.com

DMC: www.dmc.com

Die Cuts with a View: www.dcwv.com

Doodlebug: www.doodlebug.com

Duncan Crafts (Tulip Paint): www.duncancrafts.com

Dymo: www.dymo.com

EK Success: www.eksuccess.com

Ellison: www.ellison.com

Fiskars: www.fiskars.com

Fontwerks: www.fontwerks.com

Glitterex: www.glitterex.com

Glue Dots: www.gluedots.com

Hambly Screen Prints: www.hamblyscreenprints.com

Heidi Swapp: www.heidiswapp.com

Hero Arts: www.heroarts.com

Hewlett-Packard: www.hp.com

Inkadinkado: www.inkadinkado.com

Junkitz: www.junkitz.com

K&Company: www.kandcompany.com

Karen Foster: www.karenfosterdesign.com

Kilz: www.kilz.com

KI Memories: www.kimemories.com

Li'l Davis Designs: www.lildavisdesigns.com

Making Memories: www.makingmemories.com

Malabrigo: www.malabrigo.com

Manos del Uruguay: www.manos.com.uy

Marvy Uchida: www.uchida.com

May Arts: www.mayarts.com

Me and My Big Ideas: www.meandmybigideas.com

Microsoft: www.microsoft.com

My Mind's Eye: www.mymindseye.com

Offray: www.offray.com

Paper Salon: www.papersalon.com

Paper Source: www.paper-source.com

Pebbles Inc: www.pebblesinc.com

Posh Impressions: www.poshimpressions.com

Ranger Ink: www.rangerink.com

Rust-Oleum: www.rustoleum.com

Savvy Stamps: www.savvystamps.com

Scenic Route Paper Co.: www.scenicroutepaper.com

Scrapsupply: www.scrapsupply.com

Scrapworks: www.scrapworks.com

Stampendous: www.stampendous.com

Tombow: www.tombowusa.com

Tsukineko: www.tsukineko.com

Two Peas in a Bucket: www.twopeasinabucket.com

TypeNow: www.typenow.net/s.htm

Urban Lily: www.urbanlily.com

Waverly: www.waverly.com

Westrim Crafts: www.westrimcrafts.com

Contributors

DEBORAH BOLER

Debi Boler is on the design team for Scrapsupply.com and the creative team for DesignerDigitals.com and Scrapbookbling.com. She has been published in *Creating Keepsakes*, *Making Memories*, and *Scrapbook Trends*. Debi lives in California.

CANDICE CRUZ

Candice Cruz has a passion for celebrating memories through photography and scrapbooking. Her other hobbies include card making, cooking, knitting, and jewelry making. Her layouts and greeting cards have been published in several magazines and idea books. To see her work, visit www.shortcakescraps.com. Candice lives in Massachusetts, where she is a store manager at Spark Craft Studios.

RENÉE DEBLOIS

Crafty since her Girl Scout years, Renée DeBlois first focused on scrapbooking, cross-stitching, rubber-stamping, and card making. More recently, she has taken to knitting, otherwise known as collecting yarn. Renée is drawn to geometric modern art and anything black and white. As a novice fiction writer, she has started using scrapbooking and journaling as a way to develop characters and ideas. She teaches papercrafting classes and has had cards published in *Cards* and *Paper Crafts* magazines. Renée lives in New Orleans.

KIMBERLY KESTI

Kim Kesti considers herself addicted to papercrafting. Since she was a little girl, Kim has been playing with paper and glue, and today she enjoys scrapbooking and card making. She likes to use her hobby to bring a little joy to those around her. Kim lives in Arizona.

SUSAN WEINROTH

Susan Weinroth has been scrapbooking since 2000. She loves that scrapbooking and papercrafts allow her to combine both artistic creativity and photography to document the important memories in life. Susan lives in Minnesota with her family.

WENDY WHITE

Wendy White owns and operates Scrapsupply, an online scrapbook store. Wendy has been making cards for four years and enjoys discovering new techniques and products. Wendy has an online gallery of her cards and other creations at www.scrapsupply.com. She is a happily married, 35-year-old mother of three children ages eight, six, and five.

Acknowledgments

The authors would like to thank the staff of Spark Craft Studios, whose talent and enthusiasm for crafts are an inspiration to us; our husbands and families, whose love and support allows us to do work that is meaningful and fun; and all of our readers, whose continuing interest in crafting makes books like *Love Notes* possible.

Author Biographies

SPARK CRAFT STUDIOS,™ INC., located near Boston, is a stylish, modern spin on the traditional craft store. Cofounded in 2005 by Jan Stephenson and Amy Appleyard, the upscale store and studio offers a full range of craft supplies and a lounge area where crafters can meet, work, and socialize. Spark has been featured in *Time*, *Business Week Online*, the *Boston Globe*, *DailyCandy*, *Lucky*, and more. The company's founders have won awards for innovative retailing and plan to expand Spark Craft Studios to additional locations.

JAN STEPHENSON stewards Spark Craft Studios' creative vision, long-term strategic goals, and business development. Before launching Spark, she worked on marketing and fundraising campaigns for prominent nonprofit organizations. Jan received a B.A. in journalism from Ithaca College and an M.B.A. degree from Boston University.

AMY APPLEYARD manages Spark's operations, including finance, accounting, and technology. Prior to cofounding Spark, she managed her own theatrical lighting design company based out of New York, which allowed her to work with theater and opera companies all over the United States. Amy received a B.A. in theatre arts from Virginia Tech and an M.B.A. degree from Boston University.

Project Gallery

I Am Nuts for You by Candice Cruz

Sweet by Kimberly Kesti

I Love You Bunches by Debi Boler

Love is All You Need by Candice Cruz

This Heart Belongs to You by Wendy White

Oh Baby by Candice Cruz

Us 2 by Renée DeBlois

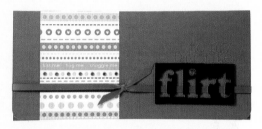

To My Favorite Flirt by Candice Cruz

Love Rocks by Candice Cruz

I Do by Wendy White

XO by Debi Boler

Love Your Laugh, Love Your Style by Candice Cruz

Index

A

Adhesives, 14

Angel Card, 70-71, 117

Attachments, 15

B

Be Silly, 36-37, 116

Boler, Debi, cards by
    I Love You Bunches, 126
    XO, 127

Bone folder, 15

Brother, 86-87, 118

Brothers and sisters, cards for, 78-89

Butterfly Kisses, 67-69, 117

C

Card stock, 14

Children, cards for, 62-77

Coloring instruments, 14

Computer and printer, 15

Cruz, Candice, cards by
    Be Silly, 36-37, 116
    For You, Mom, with Love, 98-99, 119
    Grandma Card, 92-93, 118
    Gravitation Is Not Responsible, 42-43, 116
    Heartfelt Wishes, 104-105, 119
    I Am Nuts for You, 126
    Love and Chocolate, 108-109, 119
    Love Is All You Need, 126
    Love Your Laugh, Love Your Style, 127
    Oh Baby!, 32-33, 115, 126
    To My Favorite Flirt, 127
    Top 10 Reasons Why I Love You, Sis, 84-85, 118
    To the Best Grandpa, 94-95, 118
    Who I Love, 110-111, 119
    With U I Can Just Be Me, 30-31, 115
    Woody Allen Quotation, 54-55, 117
    XOXO, 56-57, 117
    You Bring Out the Best in Me, 102-103, 119
    You Rock, 127

Cutting systems and punches, 15

D

Dad, My Hero, 96-97, 118

DeBlois, Renée, cards by
    Dad, My Hero, 96-97, 118

Happy 5th Anniversary, 40-41, 116

Happy Birthday, 64-66, 117

I'm Smitten, 50-53, 117

Love Potion #9, 28-29, 115

Red Sox, 88-89, 118

Sister Purse Box, 80-83, 118

The Heart Has Its Reasons, 60-61, 117

Us 2, 127

You Brighten My Days, Son, 72-73, 117

E

Embellishments, 15

Envelopes and templates, 14

Expressions of love, 112-113

Eyelet-setting tools, 15

F

Flying High Up on the Wings of Love, 20-21, 115

For You, Mom, with Love, 98-99, 119

Friends, cards for, 100-111

G

Glues, 14

Grandma Card, 92-93, 118

Grandparents, see Parents and grandparents, cards for

Gravitation Is Not Responsible, 42-43, 116

Greetings and sentiments, 112

H

Handwriting, 113

Happy 5th Anniversary, 40-41, 116

Happy Birthday, 64-66, 117

Heartfelt Wishes, 104-105, 119

Heart Has Its Reasons, 60-61, 117

Hole punches, 15

Hot Stuff, 44-45, 116

I

I Am Nuts for You, 126

I Do, 127

I Love You Bunches, 126

I'm Smitten, 50-53, 117

Ink and stamps, 14

In Love There Is No Measure of Time, 34-35, 116

K

Kesti, Kimberly, cards by
    Flying High Up on the Wings of Love, 20-21, 115
    In Love There Is No Measure of Time, 34-35, 116
    Love, 48-49, 116
    Sweet, 126
    True Love, 46-47, 116

You Color My World, 76-77, 118

You Have My Heart Tied Up with Love, 38-39, 116

L

Li'l Love Bug, 74-75, 118

Love, 48-49, 116

Love and Chocolate, 108-109, 119

Love Grows, 22-23, 115

Love is All You Need, 126

Love notes, 8-11
    expressions of love for, 112-113
    mailing of, 113
    materials, tools, supplies for, 12-15, 115-120

Love Potion #9, 28-29, 115

Lovers, cards for, 16-61

Love Your Laugh, Love Your Style, 127

M

Mailing regulations, 113

Materials and tools, 12-15
    detailed supply lists, 115-119
    suppliers of, 120

My Heart Belongs to You, 126

N

Note cards, blank, 14

O

Oh Baby!, 32-33, 115, 126

P

Paper and paper substitutes, 14

Paper trimmers, 15

Parents and grandparents, cards for, 90-99

Postal regulations, 113

Printer and computer, 15

Punches, 15

Q

Quotations, 113

R

Red Sox, 88-89, 118

Ribbon and trimmings, 14

Rub-ons, 14

S

Scissors, 15

Sewing machine, 15

Siblings, see Brothers and sisters, cards for

Sister Purse Box, 80-83, 118

Sisters, see Brothers and sisters, cards for

Stamps and ink, 14

Stickers, 14

Suppliers, 120

Supply lists, 115-119

Sweet, 126

T

Templates, for envelopes, 14

The Heart Has Its Reasons, 60-61, 117

To-Do List, 58-59, 117

To My Favorite Flirt, 127

Tools, see Materials and tools

Top 10 Reasons Why I Love You, Sis, 84-85, 118

To the Best Grandpa, 94-95, 118

Trimmings and ribbon, 14

True Love, 46-47, 116

U

Us 2, 127

W

Weinroth, Susan, cards by
    Hot Stuff, 44-45, 116
    Li'l Love Bug, 74-75, 118
    You Make My World Brighter, 106-107, 119
    Your Love Brings Color to My World, 26-27, 115

Where I Go, 24-25, 115

White, Wendy, cards by
    Angel Card, 70-71, 118
    Brother, 86-87, 118
    Butterfly Kisses, 67-69, 117
    I Do, 127
    Love Grows, 22-23, 115
    My Heart Belongs to You, 126
    To-Do List, 58-59, 117
    Where I Go, 24-25, 115
    You Complete Me, 18-19, 115

Who I Love, 110-111, 119

With U I Can Just Be Me, 30-31, 115

Woody Allen Quotation, 54-55, 117

Writing instruments, 14

X

XO, 127

XOXO, 56-57, 117

Y

You Brighten My Days, Son, 72-73, 117

You Bring Out the Best in Me, 102-103, 119

You Color My World, 76-77, 118

You Complete Me, 18-19, 115

You Have My Heart Tied Up with Love, 38-39, 116

You Make My World Brighter, 106-107, 119

Your Love Brings Color to My World, 26-27, 115

You Rock, 127